AF887457

THE FUN ENTREPRENEURS HAVE

with Free-Market Systems & Principles

by

Robert E. Sonntag, President

Philomod® Institute

Silent E Publishing Company
4446 Hendricks Ave, #141
Jacksonville, FL 32207

ISBN-10: 0-9755104-8-7

ISBN-13: 978-0-9755104-8-3

1 2 3 4 5 6 7 8

This book is dedicated to my wonderful daughter, Julia S. Daze. She could read my mind and always knew exactly what to draw. You will see her illustrations throughout this book.

Table of Contents

Introduction

From the Declaration of Independence:

"We hold these truths to be self-evident..."

Not necessarily. To a man of Thomas Jefferson's intelligence: Yes, they were self-evident. But to the average citizen? No. Not all persons of average intelligence found the ideas of Philadelphia's Constitutional Convention to be *self-evident.*

The purpose of the "*Federalist Papers*," 85 articles written by Alexander Hamilton, John Jay, and James Madison in 1787-1788 was to explain to the American people what had been written in Philadelphia in 1787. *Did the people understand the new Constitution? Did they get it?* These men were concerned. Their "papers" were to *explain and clarify.*

In the 1980's it became evident that the American people had still *not gotten it. If they had, they would have been making better decisions at their voting booths.*

Today we know the average American has an IQ of 100, somewhere between 70 and 130. *That is the norm.* Half of us have IQs above 100, and we can vote. *Also half of us have IQ's below 100, and can also vote.*

In this book we have taken new steps to help *everyone* get the ideas of the Constitutional Convention. Here we offer Americans *drawings and copyrighted blueprints of three-dimensional models. These models summarize the meanings of two opposing political-economic systems and the individual structures of 14 principles.* Simply stated there are two Opposing Systems and 14 Principles at work.

After 225 years, we set out once again to clarify. One might say that this book offers *Federalist Structures* as supplements to the *Federalist Papers.*

Philomods® are "models of philosophies." Their *structures clarify political, economic, and management* concepts for those who may not have fully grasped these concepts.

We want, as Hamilton, Jay, and Madison wanted, for all Americans to understand the principles of freedom and of force that govern our lives.

Philomod Institute®

Robert E. Sonntag, President

The Sonntags, the Kinkeads, & the Combination

The Sonntags, 1890-2010

Every American family has its comfort zone. Rather than trying to describe it, let me show you a rough map of our family's comfort zone. This will save us a lot of time. You will have become quickly acquainted with our territory.

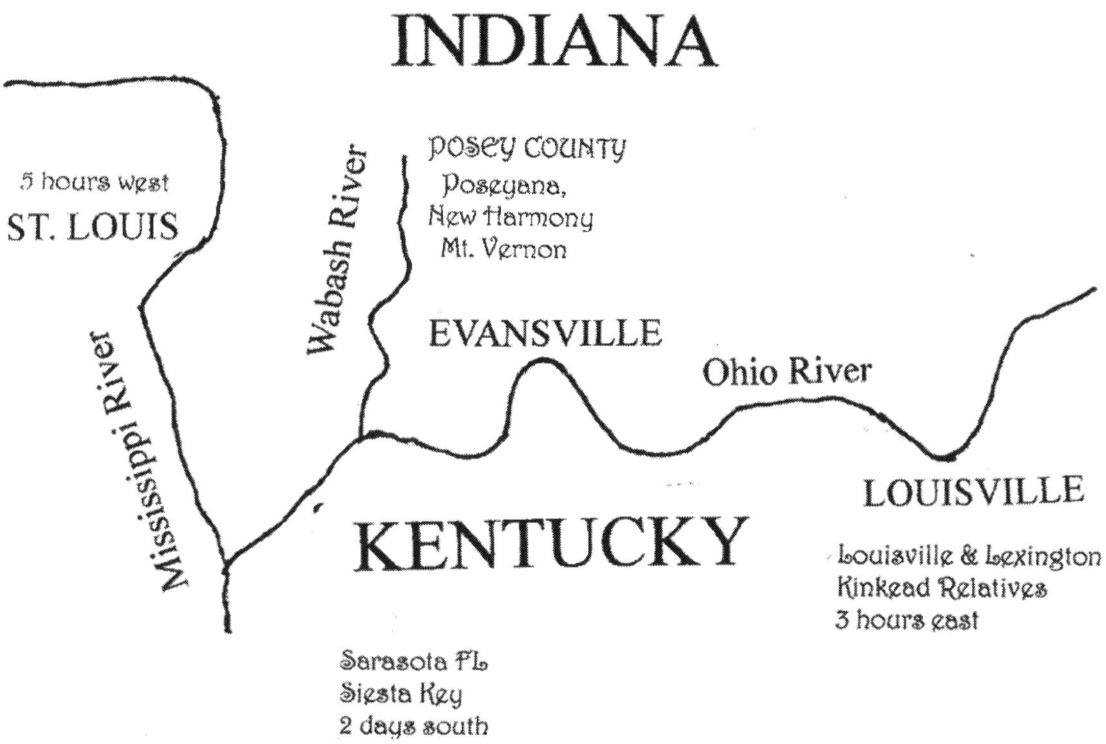

Ed Sonntag, my father, was born in 1890, in Evansville in an America that was in excellent, vibrant health. This year, 2011, 120 years have passed. Our great United States of America is a very sick country. Over this 120-year period our America slowly declined in health because someone had slipped its people this one new idea: "All you have to do to improve the situation is ask the government."

That's it.

Prior to 1890, Americans were free from this simple idea. Americans, faced with a situation that they thought needed to be improved, rolled up their sleeves and said "Let's tackle this situation." That's what the Founders did. It's what responsible parents had always done.

"Ask the government to improve the situation." Does that idea sound alien to you today? I doubt it. I doubt that you would even pause to consider this an especially dangerous idea. I doubt that you realize as a stand-alone idea this is deadly poison. It packs an unimaginable punch of nation-killing damage.

Once that new idea got its nose under the edge of the tent, it gained acceptability, even respectability in some quarters, and we began our own destruction. We did it ourselves to ourselves. It took nothing more. General acceptance came about slowly, then gained momentum. "Hey, old buddy, the government should help us here." "Of course. What a good idea. Why didn't I think of that?" And the deadly infection was implanted somewhere in an American brain.

Step One of the Choosing Process is "Improve the situation." Step Two: "Choices come in twos or more. A choice of one is force." When the choice becomes government's choice, it becomes sheer force. Brace yourself. You are to hear a lot about the "Ten Characteristics of Choice." The ten characteristics of choice are based upon one principle: "Our Individual Freedom to Choose." It was our Founding Fathers' idea, and our Declaration of Independence and our Constitution are based on it.

But I rush too quickly into principles. Let's not rush.

I'd like to tell you a family story. It is the story of my father, Ed Sonntag, of Evansville, a world-class salesman with an impressive list of credits. He married Polly

Kinkead of Louisville, a bright, red-headed artist who became a widely recognized and acclaimed entrepreneur. Salesman teams up with artist. A little story that will illustrate some of the principles you need to know about the free-market American philosophy.

The Sonntags

Looking back at the Sonntag family male mind over several generations, I am pleased to report that it seems to have simple but firm qualities that reappear rather regularly. The right lobe in our brains seems blessed with a rather high degree of imagination and is rather good at synthesis. Our left lobes seem to enjoy taking new ideas from its neighbor lobe and applying the necessary reason and logic to bring forth favorable results.

These are the minds of salesmen and of entrepreneurs, not in the least complicated or profound. Everyday serviceable, you might say. A thousand miles from Pittsburgh to the mouth of the Ohio, another thousand to New Orleans, the Ohio and Mississippi Rivers were the *Interstate System of the nineteenth century.* The Sonntags were at the midway point. John Haviland Sonntag, 1837-1898, father of the five Sonntag brothers of Evansville, was a "drummer." After the Civil War he was a salesman for the Belknap Hardware Company of Louisville. His territory was the Mississippi River, with all its tributaries from Minneapolis down to New Orleans 1,500 miles to the south. In the fall of each year John covered his territory using the Mississippi River and Missouri River steamboats and stepped ashore to write his orders at each of his hundreds of retail hardware stores. In the spring of the following year Belknap Hardware delivered the hundreds of orders by steamboat that John had written the fall before.

At some point John added the Blount Plough Company to his Belknap Hardware representation. Thus one additional new product that he launched in his territory was the moldboard plough. This was the new sharp steel blade the team of mules pulled to cut a clean 18-inch furrow in the fertile American plains. John was responsible for distributing this product into the South and western US. Its value? He *improved the situation, enhanced the productivity* for millions of American farmers.

John Haviland Sonntag Sr.
Father of Five Brothers
B. November 21, 1837, Cincinnati, OH
D. June 5, 1898, Evansville IN

Ellen Brennan Sonntag
Mother of the Five Brothers
B. March 1, 1835, Ireland
D. June 11, 1888, Evansville, IN

John was a dude. He wore fine wool suits with a vest. Under each arm he carried a six-gun. Riverboats after the Civil War? Rough, tough travelers, many ex-Confederates, not happy with the outcome of their war with the North. My father said simply: "John Sonntag was one tough buzzard."

John H. Sonntag's birth year was 1837. Mark Twain (Samuel L Clemens) was born in 1835. There is no reason to believe that the two ever met. However, Twain's *Life on the Mississippi,* should you choose to read it, provides a nostalgic insight into those riverboat days. *River pilots carefully easing their great paddle-wheel boats up the big river in the dead darkness of night. No shoreline lights or channel lights. That was adventure!*

John was tough but apparently a gentleman and good father. John and his Irish wife, Ellen Brennan Sonntag, 1835-1888, raised five strapping boys. Up until the 1930s these Sonntag brothers were a commercial force in their city, by then, population 90,000.

Ellen, born in Ireland, never lost her brogue. My father said that until the day she died she talked like she never got off the boat. I don't know that the five boys were easy to rear. One example, remembered by my grandfather: At one point the five boys were provided with new Levi trousers. All five hated the pants. They improved the situation. "To wear the trousers out as quickly as possible, we rubbed on the knees with bricks until they were completely worn through and had to be replaced."

On your map of the USA put your finger on Minneapolis way up there on the Mississippi River. Now imagine a north-south line running from that point north to Canada and straight south to the Gulf of Mexico. That line, very roughly demarked the "western frontier of the USA" in the 1870s and 80s. That was the time of Mark Twain's wonderful 1,800-mile stage coach trip from Joplin, Missouri to Carson City, Nevada, as told in *"Roughing It."* When headed west out of Joplin, "you left the States." *You left the USA!"*

Joplin was the western frontier of John H. Sonntag's territory. Now doesn't that make my great grandfather a "Western frontier man?" And the five Sonntag brothers "frontier boys," like Twain's Tom Sawyer? Sure it does. Able to show the neighborhood boys how much fun it is to paint a fence. That's how I'd like you to see them.

Like the wives of all traveling salesmen Ellen had to bring up the boys almost by herself. The lady deserves our applause. I like to think that Ellen's Irish genes gave five stolid German boys a real kick in the britches. With a German ability to plan and an Irish talent for spinning stories they were given two entrepreneurial talents.

Left to Right: Edward Francis (1862-1934), John Haviland Jr. (1866- 1930), George Walker (1871-1939), William Louis (1860-?), Marcus Smith (1859-1936).

Mark became the banker. Walker was the realtor. Edward, my grandfather, was the contractor. I'm not sure what Will did. John went off to California, and his son, Jack, later helped produce the "*M.A.S.H*" series for TV.

Three of the brothers had fine homes on Riverside Drive or SE First Street, and most days they walked home from their businesses for lunch.

For the first third of the twentieth century, the Sonntag brothers and their wives dominated the Evansville business and social scene. During the 1920's and 30's when I was a boy in Evansville, I learned that all the four corners of Sixth and Main were family corners, part of the original Evansville land grant.

On the northwest corner stood Mark's American Trust Bank. On the northeast corner of the quadrant there was the five-story Sonntag Hotel.

At street level was the grand marquee of Loew's Victory Theater. This opulent motion picture theater, typical of the booming twenties, was complete with crystal chandeliers and bronze statues in the lobby and golden carvings around the presidium. The best movies played here. The massive oil landscape paintings of the Catskills by William Louis Sonntag (1822-1900) of the Hudson River Art Group decked the walls of the lobby, each with its little brass lamp shining on it. These masterpieces were owned by Uncle Mark, William Louis's nephew. Over the years they became quite valuable and passed outside the family. In the late 1920s Mark was named president of the American Bankers Association and the following year was elected Mayor of Evansville.

By the 1950's the old theater had closed and the old Sonntag Hotel had sunk to a shabby state. By then it was sometimes referred to as the "biggest red-light house on Main Street."

On the northeast corner of Sixth & Main was Gueiss's Restaurant which extended back to the alley. Behind Gueiss's across the alley was my grandfather's business, the E. F. Sonntag Tile & Mantle Co. The fireplace and hearth in those days were the family center of the fine home. No radio, no TV, the place to meet was at the fireside in the living room. There was usually a piano nearby. As a boy my father learned to play, and learned to sing in the boys choir at the Episcopal Church. Perhaps we will have a chance to highlight his musical talents later in our story.

On the fourth corner stood Ed's two-story store which late in the 20's became the F. W. Woolworth Company. The Woolworth store was a helpful asset for my father. The rent they paid helped him pull up stakes during the depression and move his wife Polly, my brother Bill and myself to Sarasota in 1936. They had been making exploratory trips to find a new place to settle. I had attended third grade in McAllen, Texas and my fifth in Delray Beach, Florida.

But let's return to my dad in his earlier years, when the salesman-entrepreneur personality first became evident. My father, the first Sonntag to have a college education, graduated Purdue University in 1912, and he had a plan. Immediately he shipped off to Havana Cuba. The objective: Learn to speak Spanish fluently.

He became a "greeter" for one of Havana's big hotels. His job was to drive the hotel coach (horse-drawn or gasoline powered?) to Havana harbor each day and there to welcome the guests coming into Havana from all over the world for the Cuban cuisine, the gambling, and the senoritas. He helped them from their ships, looked after their safety and their luggage, and hauled them off to the hotel, where he then served as their concierge. After a year of this, he had the Spanish language down cold. He had *improved his situation.*

In 1913 his plan took him to Akron, Ohio, home of the Goodyear Tire and Rubber Company, at the time just 16 years in business. There he introduced himself to Frank Seiberling, the founder and president of the company. “Sir, I would like to be your representative in South America and establish the new Goodyear pneumatic tire on the southern continent, I am an engineer from Purdue University and I speak fluent Spanish." Seiberling hired him.

Over the next three years he established Goodyear solidly in Argentina, Brazil, Chile, Peru, and Ecuador. And his stories of that time entertained us for years. Ed was amazed at the stamina of the little Peruvian Indian guides who could carry 60 pounds on their backs over 12,000-foot high mountain trails where Ed could barely breath. He never forgot the horrible conditions in Guayaquil, Ecuador, "a stinking city with drunken sailors on every corner and no place for a drummer to find a decent meal." The complaints by some Goodyear customers that the pedals on their tractors got hot and burned the soles of their bare feet brought forth a small new Goodyear product: rubber covers for tractor pedals. And Rio. "Rio de Janeiro was the most beautiful city in the world and still is."

Then he had to return home. The US Army beckoned. Before he left Buenos Aires, he went to a tailor and had a special vest made. It had concealed pockets that would hide several gold coins. He felt that the voyage home may have held hazards: Toughs aboard ship, Caribbean hurricanes, German U-boats.

Edward M. Sonntag, age 27, Home from South America, 1917

Ed was lucky. Luck has so often helped our family. The lives of American Army first lieutenants in the trenches of France were known to be short-lived. The war ended before he had to ship out. But he almost died of the Spanish flu. The point is: *He had a plan and he executed his plan.* Without missing a beat, at age 29 he had become the star salesman of a new American corporation.

The Kinkeads

In 1919 Ed improved the situation when he married Polly Kinkead, a redheaded artist from Louisville, a graduate of New York's Parsons School of Design.

We diverge for a moment with a Louisville side story. Robert Kinkead, Polly's father, was a Louisville judge. When he asked his daughter Polly if she wanted to be a Louisville debutante, she said no, she wanted to study art, and off she went, age 17, to Parsons. Now Polly had an older brother, Cleves, another strong-minded redhead. Judge Kinkead wanted his son Cleves to be a lawyer and sent him off to Harvard and then the University of Virginia, School of Law. Cleves returned home to Louisville, but didn't care for the law. In fact he hated the law. Cleves had to *improve his situation.*

So Cleves wrote a play. He named it "*Common Clay*" and it enjoyed one of the longest runs on Broadway until "*Tobacco Road.*" in the 1930s. Feisty Cleves then married Kitty, a beautiful Broadway showgirl (Polly said Kitty didn't have a brain in her pretty head), returned home to Louisville, settled his fanny in a big easy chair at the posh Pendennis Club to read the daily Courier-Journal and never worked another lick in his life.

Left: Cleves at 27, the year he wrote *"Common Clay"* Right: Cleves at age 60

The thrilling connection here is that when Polly, at age 17, trotted off to New York to the Parsons School, there in lights eight feet high on Broadway, was the sign: *"Common Clay, by Cleves Kinkead."* Imagine the reception this little Kentucky Kinkead girl got when she walked in the front door at Parsons.

The Combination

In January 1919 Polly and Ed left on their honeymoon for the port of Cadiz, Spain to establish Goodyear in Europe. One little incident dented the honeymoon voyage at sea. To celebrate when they left New York, they bought a big chunk of camembert cheese. After two days at sea the camembert became very smelly, so they threw it out their cabin's porthole. The ocean breeze did not favor them. The smelly cheese stuck to and dribbled down the ship's side. When they wanted a little fresh air in their cabin, they had to endure the stench. "Once you have the Spanish," Ed always said, "the French, Portuguese and Italian come easy." So Ed sold tires while Polly enjoyed the great art galleries of Paris, Madrid, Florence and Venice.

In 1922, the great Goodyear European adventure ended. They were living in Madrid. Polly was expecting a baby in October. They didn't want me to be a Spaniard.

Time to come home. The job was done. There were Goodyear tires in every city and village from the northern coasts of France down through Spain and Portugal to the Rock of Gibraltar. And to the east throughout Italy to the tip of its boot in the Mediterranean Sea.

And Polly. She had had the opportunity to study the great masters in Madrid's El Prado, the Paris Louvre and the galleries of Florence, and Venice. Kentucky had covered thoroughly the best Europe had to offer. Her favorite? In El Prado the fine portraits of Francisco Goya. And now she spoke fluent French and Spanish.

They were America's ambassadors. They wanted to meet the natives and they did. When in later winters in their retirement years they traveled back to France and Spain from Evansville they found some of their old friends were still there.

In 1923, in eight years, one young man, age 32, single-handedly, had put two continents in the pocket of the young 22-year old Goodyear Company... South America, then Europe. He had improved that young company's situation. He had taken the Goodyear Tire and Rubber Company *global.*

Family Portrait 1923. Polly is 27, Ed is 33 and I am about three months.

Many years later American industry would find itself talking a lot about *the new concept of "global."* One young salesman from Indiana had *been there and done "global"* 80 years before. If, being *global,* Ed was 80 years ahead of his time, his mother Jeanne was 100 years ahead with her 1915 "Electric."

Jeanie Sonntag & Electric, 1918

These cars were top heavy from the weight of their batteries and were known to tip over going around corners. But Jeanie, wife of an entrepreneur had her fun. When encountering her "female discomforts," this tea-totaling lady turned for relief to "Peruna," never realizing her patent medicine was 90% alcohol. So let's picture this: possibly Evansville's first DUI: Tipsy Jeanie, trying to turn city corners in her tipsy Electric. But back to our more recent family story.

In their retirement years back home in Evansville, to maintain their language skills, Polly and Ed spoke only Spanish to each other on Mondays, Wednesdays and

Fridays and only French on Tuesdays, Thursdays, and Saturdays. When brother Bill and I were growing up, they conversed in Spanish whenever they didn't want us kids to know what the hell they were talking about.

As for "global," we will return to that subject in the last chapter.

In Four Generations of One Family

Why have I chosen to build our story around the Sonntag family? Because the story of our family's lives has been woven in with outstanding sales skills, luck, and successful entrepreneurial efforts. In four generations of one family, the lives of eight members have been centered on selling and entrepreneurship. It's what we did and do. Two salesmen, John H. and Edward M., covered ten thousand-square-mile territories and produced outstanding results: John: thousands upon thousands of square miles of the rugged American frontier by steamboat. Ed: utilizing an acquired comfort with four languages, covered thousands of square miles on the frontiers of South America and then the great nations of Western Europe.

There were six entrepreneurs over three generations of the family: Mark, Walker, Edward F., John, Polly, and myself. We six were lucky enough to visualize, conceive, start, and manage our own successful businesses.

College professors teach about 1) the American free-market system, and 2) the entrepreneurship skills that must build and maintain that system. Most have never left their college classrooms. We are amazed they can teach the subject at all. They have certainly missed the fun of it.

Things You Should Know About Being an Entrepreneur

This year, 2011, the US is at 9% unemployment. Where must growth come from? New ideas. New products. *New entrepreneurs. These are the fountainheads. These are the people who will improve the situation. It is disappointing that this truth is not more generally accepted.* Let me build upon this.

- Being an entrepreneur almost satisfies your very soul. It's that much fun.
- You can't wait to get there in the morning and improve the situation. (Actually your brain never went home last night.)
- Your customers may drive you nuts. Grin and bear it.
- You pity people who have to work for others, and try to remember that when dealing with your own people.
- Other entrepreneurs are usually the people you like best.
- Opportunity knocks? *Never. Opportunity is not that blatant.* Opportunity creeps up beside you in the fog and stands 17 feet off to your right but slightly behind you. *Sneaky. Quiet.* It is the entrepreneur who senses a "felt uneasiness" (Thank you, Ludwig von Mises, for that *essential* phrase.) The entrepreneur turns his head. Ah, yes it's there. A new idea in its shapeless, before-birth form. The entrepreneur smiles and walks toward it. *An enterprise may have been conceived today.*

People who do not understand entrepreneurship miss so much. They may even become political adversaries, simply because they are deaf to the heartbeat of America.

The Posey-ana Shop
Polly Sonntag's 25-Year Successful Enterprise in Furniture Design & Decoration: Fun, Paint, and Profits

It was a forty-seven acre square of Indiana farmland. Across the north border and down the western border were gravel roads. Defining the perimeter were split rail fences. In the very northwestern corner, the highest point of the land, there were three buildings. The old barn sat on the corner where the two roads met. A 16 x 18 foot granary sat about 30 feet east of the barn. The shingle covered house was southeast of the barn and granary. The well, pump, and privy were behind the house.

The site plan, very roughly, looked like this.

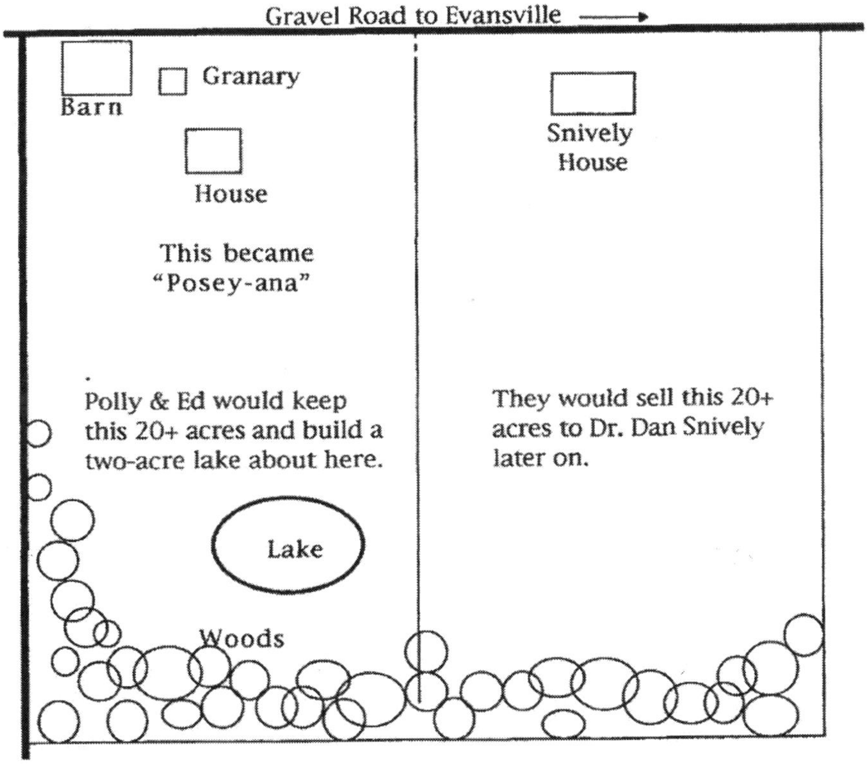

Site Plan of 47 acres in Posey County

Posey County Indiana lies adjacent to and west of Vanderburgh County whose seat is Evansville. It is the southwestern most county in Indiana. Posey County is bordered on the west by the Wabash River, on the south by the Ohio. Leaving Evansville you drive west about nine miles to Posey-ana. Polly and Ed were still living in Chapel Hill where they had moved after Sarasota. They itched to move back to their roots. The question was: Ed's roots or Polly's?

Polly had left Louisville in 1919. Their absence from their Louisville roots was almost 30 tears. On the other hand their absence from Evansville was only ten. Indiana won. Ed phoned the Evansville realtor and bought the farm. Polly wanted to paint. Ed wanted a woodworking shop. The red barn became Polly's shop. The granary, with a big plate glass window added, became Ed's workshop.

The house. Beneath the shingles were two log cabins with a "breezeway" between. The oak and poplar floorboards were 14, sometimes 16 inches wide. Ed reduced the size of the kitchen to make a small modern bathroom. No more privy. One cabin became their bedroom, the other the living room with its fireplace. From the outside it still appeared as a unit, a simple shingle house.

Posey-ana in the snow. Note split rail fence.
These fences were throughout the property and
provided exactly the right touch.

George and Albion Smith were best friends and also had a country home north of downtown Evansville. George was a stockbroker, but energetic, wiry, did his own yard work. One Saturday morning he was out front cutting his grass--dirty, sweaty, and smelly.

A stranger stopped. George stops the mower. "Good morning!" said the stranger. "I have a place not far from here and need someone to cut the grass, trim the shrubs, maybe clean the gutters. What kind of pay do you get?" George looks the stranger in the eye. "I don't get paid. The lady who lives here lets me sleep with her."

Ed had a little 3-acre lake built about 50 yards from the house and he built a dock. He named it "Loch Stock-n-barrel." Summers we swam. Winters we ice skated. We learned how to ice skate by putting a dining room chair on the ice and scooting it around until we were skilled enough to turn loose.

The Posey-ana Shop. They shoveled the manure out of the barn, laid down an attractive old brick floor, and Ed built shelving. This red barn became the base of Polly's new business.

She Had Found The Answer

And this became their routine. On week-ends they attended farm auctions all over southern Indiana and northern Kentucky. Polly was looking for old wooden wardrobes, armoires, cabinets, chests, dressers, pie safes and even washtubs she could decorate in her Posey-ana style. That style was sort of "Pennsylvania Dutch" but distinctive through her own unique el Prado touches.

Ed was scouting for old lumber, poplar and walnut, much of it 16, 18 even 24 inches wide. When an old Indiana barn is razed, it might yield pine, walnut, or poplar. Some of these planks could well have been a part of the virgin forest that covered the land from the Atlantic Ocean to the Mississippi River. These planks became tabletops on the country-style tables Ed built in his workshop. They would fill the Plymouth station wagon from these Saturday farm auctions and haul all of this home to Posey-ana.

The cost of these old dressers, chests, cabinets, and wardrobes: usually 50 cents, sometimes as much as $4 or $5. When Ed was finished cleaning up and repairing these old pieces in his workshop, Polly went to work in her barn with her designs and her paints and they became "Posey-ana Pieces." Retail prices: $395 to $595. Ed would say, "Polly, I don't know how long you can get away with this." But they did for the next 20 years.

Various Posey-ana Pieces

Polly at work in Posey-ana Barn

And I liked those pieces my father created in his woodworking shop. They influenced some basic steps I took as an entrepreneur 20 years later.

Polly and Ed did "get away with it" from 1947 until they moved in town to their condo, the Posey-ana name spreading as far east as Louisville, north to Indianapolis and west to St. Louis. She *improved the situation* in hundreds of homes. We estimated that over this period Polly had decorated over 500 pieces.

On the Wabash River on the western boundary of Posey County there is situated the historic, experimental socialist community of New Harmony. Between 1825 and 1828, Robert Owen of London, England and his followers originated a form of communal living there. It failed completely. Socialism in Posey County failed. A century later in Posey County, American free enterprise *improved the situation* for all the participating parties.

In 1957, the quaint and superb restaurant, the Red Geranium, was holding its grand opening as a part of the New Harmony historical experience. It was an upscale country eating place with ambiance. Polly and Ed were invited. Aggie and I went along for the fun and food.

When we were settled at our table amidst the splendid surroundings, we ordered drinks and Ed ordered a Martini. Our sweet little country waitress returned to the table with our drinks but with an apology to Ed. "I didn't know how to make a Martini, so I just brought you this glassful of gin. Is that OK? Ed smiled sweetly at her and said, "That's *just fine*."

Toward the end of the Posey-ana era, oil was discovered in our Indiana-Kentucky area. Massive oil-drilling rigs became commonplace on the country roads. The wells with their rocker-arm pumps in Texas they're called "pump jacks", sprung up everywhere, lending the atmosphere the rich smell of Indiana crude as they pumped night and day. Geologists flocked to the area.

Evansville was the only settlement that could possibly be called a city in the center of this exciting oil strike. A posh Petroleum Club was formed and had its lavish dining room on the top floor of the Old National Bank Building downtown. And Posey-ana suddenly had its own oil well! What excitement! The well produced 200 barrels the first week. Ed ordered a new tuxedo from Brooks Brothers. The second week production dropped to 90 barrels. When an offset well, required by law, was drilled on Dr. Dan Snively's property next door, Posey-ana's production dropped to 25 barrels. The producers shut down the well pump.

The upshot of our family oil story is that when Ed received his check from the oil producer, it was almost the exact amount as the new Brooks tux. Dr. Dan Snively, who bought the eastern half the original 47 acres was our Medical Director at Mead Johnson & Co. He was one of America's most noted nutritionists and designed the simplest reducing diet I have ever known.

It provides 1,000 calories and 60 grams of protein. It's balanced:

One pound of cottage cheese

All the leafy greens you care to eat

One multiple-vitamin pill

Three bottles of beer

It helps a heap if you really like cottage cheese.

Management Training
Mead Johnson & Co.
A 13-Year Corporate Training Course in Modern Marketing

I was at the McCurdy Hotel bar after work at the Evansville Press, where I was paid $30 a week to sell newspaper advertising. The problem was that I was spending $40 a week on beer and dates. A fine looking businessman, a little older than myself, took the seat next to me. He introduced himself as Jack Schaup and we struck up a conversation. Soon the question came around to, "What do you do?" I told him I sold advertising for the local newspaper. "And what do you do?"

"I'm with Mead Johnson," Schaup answered. "My territory's in Texas, and I'm up here for a sales meeting, I really like Mead. We call on physicians, mostly pediatricians, because our product line includes a lot of baby foods. You've heard of Pablum. Doctors like our company because we are 100 percent 'ethical.' That means we never advertise to the public. That assures the doctor full control in his relationship with his patients, a situation he likes. Our ethical code of silence is probably the reason that even folks here in Evansville may not know exactly what Mead does."

More talk, then he asked, "Why don't you come out to the company and talk with Bill Larson, our sales manager? We're always looking for good young men."

And I did. I called Mr. Larson, told his secretary that I had met Jack Schaup, and Jack suggested I meet her boss. I was given an appointment just two days away. I walked into Bill Larson's office and he asked, "Any relation to Ed Sonntag?" I said I was his son. "Ed and I golf together," he said. (Wow.)

"Bob, I'd like to bring in our medical director to ask you a few questions," he said.

"It helps if you have a little knowledge of medicine." (Not so wow.)

Dr. Dan Snively came into Larson's office, and we were introduced. Dan said, "We like to hire pharmacists. We are ethical pharmaceutical manufacturers. But we frequently hire young laymen, and we can teach them much of what they need in our sales training course. What are the symptoms of pellagra?"

The symptoms of pellagra? My God! Then, something very, very lucky happened. From a biology course many years before I just happened to remember: "Diarrhea, dermatitis, and dementia," I answered. Luckeee!

Dan Snively turned to Bill Larson and said, "He'll do." and left the office. My employment interview was over. My territory would be southern West Virginia. Headquarters: Charleston.

In Charleston I met my future wife, Aggie, Agnes Arbuckle Jefferds. Joseph Jefferds, Sr. was Aggie's father. He was treasurer of the Kanawha Drug Company, Mead's wholesale distributor for West Virginia and Virginia. His brother, "Rob" was the company's sales manager. Aggie's Uncle Rob, years before, had built up the Kanawha Drug Company's sales by traveling the state of West Virginia on horseback. Horseback! The territory I was to cover in my Ford Rob Jefferds had covered on horseback! Believe me, I had the greatest respect for Uncle Rob. There was a salesman!

Joe Jefferds Sr., Aggie father, was Kanawha Drug Co.'s financial department, a widower and a sweet, dignified old gentleman who had raised three fine kids, a son and two daughters. A sample of his humor: "Bob, come sit down and tell me what you know. It won't take long." And "Now Bob, when you bring my daughter home tonight, if I'm not up, just lean her against the door bell."

Aggie's older brother, Joe Jr., was a graduate of MIT, an engineer and emerging entrepreneur of note. He had started his own materials handling business. (That's moving stuff inside factories whether it be by roller tracks or fork-lift truck.) At last count Joe's company served several neighboring states as well as West Virginia and had 200 employees. When Joe died in 2006 he had become in many people's eyes Charleston's outstanding citizen.

Calling on the fine physicians in the small towns of West Virginia was a pleasant experience. There was an interesting set-up in the little coal-mining towns between the local physician and the coal company. Many of the young doctors were graduates of the University of Virginia, School of Medicine. Fresh out of their residencies, they needed immediately to begin earning a living. One way to do this, while they thought about a permanent location to set up practice, was to go to work for the mining companies in the West Virginia coal towns. In my day they were paid $2 a year per coal miner. With coal miners' wives and their floor-wetting babies for patients, my doctors were always happy to take a break to talk with "the Mead man."

After a year in Charleston, Aggie and I married and we were off to Albany, New York, my new territory. And what a beautiful area: the Catskills, the Hudson River Valley towns as far south as Poughkeepsie, the Adirondack towns as far west as Utica, and north through Lake Placid, up past Lake Champlain to Plattsburgh on the Canadian border. In winter one had better learn quickly how to drive on snow and ice. I wore boots that laced almost to my knees.

Aggie and I learned how to hold a cigarette lighter under our car keys in the mornings so the keys would enter the frozen key holes of our car doors. But in summer, just a few miles east across the Massachusetts line there were the wonderful Berkshire Music Festivals with the Boston Pops. And once again, the doctors were just as welcoming as those in the coal camps. In the little towns all over upstate New York they always seemed ready to take a break from their patients to see "the Mead man."

Our son Ned was born in Albany Hospital and has been a Yankee ever since. He now lives in Harwich Massachusetts and illustrates Betty Boop for the Hearst Corporation. An old journalism major always tempted to report on the news, I liked to write about my sales experiences and often imparted sales tips to the home office in Evansville. Quite regularly they sent my stuff out to 350 other Mead salesmen in our weekly newsletter. The home office must have gotten sick of all my letters. After four years in Albany they asked me to come back to the home office in Evansville and be their sales promotion manager.

Bringing a salesman from the field into a junior marketing position means that the salesman needs training in management. Management and selling are different. At the University of North Carolina, as a journalism major, I had not taken a single course in business management. Mead used Booz Allen, the fine consultancy, to help with that training. For about nine months, Rudy Dalmeier of Booz Allen "lived with me" in my little office. Rudy taught me how to write a marketing program. And that was just the beginning. He really taught me many of my first principles of business management.

Mead Johnson taught us: "There is research, there is manufacturing, and then there is marketing. All else is secondary." Today in 2011, when the Wall Street banks are weeping and wailing, my mind returns to my early mentors: "Sorry, I say, you banks are only financial folk, neither research, nor manufacturing, nor marketing; you are secondary. Goldman Sachs? Secondary. Morgan Stanley? Secondary. I'll not be worried by the likes of you.

Neither Rudy Dalmeier, however, nor Peter Drucker (whose books on management I later devoured) ever taught me this little gem: It's a good idea for management types to learn to play golf. We had a foursome: Emmett Terrell our eastern sales manager, Lloyd Pressel, the company psychologist, and Roger Zion, our sales training manager who later became US Congressman for the Eighth District of Indiana. Sunday mornings on the Evansville Country Club course was our hour. If you never land your tee shot in the fairway, learn not to sweat it. There's the fellowship, the beautiful rolling scenery, and you may even get a little exercise.

We marketed some notable new products. Two of our most outstanding are still selling briskly 60 years later: Colace and Metrecal. Colace is a "stool softener" and it was a big new idea. Chemically sodium sulfasuccinate, it's really like a pinch of Tide detergent. It doesn't move the bowel; it just softens so that the stool passes through comfortably. We designed a clever sales device for our sales reps to use with their doctors. (This is what sales promotion managers are paid to do: Get the new product idea across to the customer accurately and very, very quickly.)

Beginning with a little glass castor (used under furniture legs to keep them from digging into carpets) we had small circles of highly compressed sponge manufactured, then cut round to fit inside the caster. Each sponge was then printed with the name "Colace." Each of these little sponges, fitted inside our little glass castors, was then impregnated with stearic acid. This meant that our little sponge in its little glass castor, when brought out by our representatives in their doctors' offices, would not absorb water.

(Our sales reps, of course, carried little bottles of water and eyedroppers for this demonstration.) But behold! When our rep added a drop of Colace to the little sponge, it swelled instantly to its regular sponge size.

We had improved the patient's situation. We had found an answer. This demonstrated instantly for our physicians that Colace immediately penetrates a fatty stool whereas normal colonic fluids may not, thus softening the stool for a comfortable BM by the patient. Doctors got the message instantly, and Mead Johnson had a new million-dollar product. The final touch was we left the little glass castor with its wet sponge as a postage-stamp wetter for the doctor's secretary. This was years before the US Post Office came out with "already-licked stamps."

Then we had Metrecal, for weight reduction, another winner. I went out calling on drug stores in the Washington DC area to get druggists' responses to this new product. One druggist I interviewed immediately picked up his phone, called his broker and ordered 100 shares of Mead Johnson stock!

At 250 calories and 15 grams of protein per glassful, plus all her daily vitamins and minerals, a fat patient received her complete nutrition in four glasses of Metrecal each day, meeting complete nutritional needs. We improved the situations quickly and simply for hundreds of thousands of obese women. One hitch soon became apparent. A few patients didn't quite understand why they were gaining, not losing weight. We discovered the problem. These fatties ate their usual three meals, then drank four glasses of Metrecal every day! But aside from such misunderstandings there was no doubt Mead Johnson had another hit.

Mead Johnson, because of Metrecal, went through real agonies about its 100%

"ethical image." Realize that some "ethical" pharmaceutical manufacturers hawk their new products in consumer magazines and on TV. To advertise to the public or not was an important decision for Mead to make. Remember, we Mead reps always received a warm welcome from our physicians because it was well known that we never advertised direct to patients. Mead improved and supported his situation by keeping the pressure off him and leaving him in one hundred percent control over his doctor-patient relationships. Thou shalt not advertise to the public was an important part of "medical ethics."

But the decision was finally made. Ladies' magazines would carry Metrecal ads. But by then the competitive advantage of the moment had passed. Very quickly giant Lever Brothers was in drug stores and grocery stores with "Slimfast." Lever improved the consumers' situation by making its product available in twice as many stores. Metrecal no longer had the market to itself and American competition was in play. Metrecal today has been bought and sold twice by other manufacturers, is now owned by Nestle, is named Boost, and is available in several useful variations.

Because of my part in these successes, Mead Johnson improved my situation. I was named Director of Vitamin Marketing. This gave me full responsibility for Mead's most profitable brand of products. I was now a "brand manager."

Early on I discovered the differing work patterns between Chicago and New York ad agencies. Agency folk in Chicago were at their desks at 9:00 in the morning. In New York, after their train commutes, they arrived at their offices at 10:00. At 11:30 they began fidgeting about lunch. At 12:00 or there-abouts they left for their two-martini lunch. At 2:00 they returned. By 4:00 they grew anxious about catching their 5:00 train back to Westchester or Connecticut. That was years ago. And today the University of

Chicago economists put all the others in the shade, and they can get to the office any time they want.

What a pain in the tail flying has become.

The Wall Street Journal, Oct. 27, 2011, ran a feature story "Return of Pan Am for a Weekend." It reminded us of the 1970's and what fun it was to fly.

As the Director for Vitamin Marketing for Mead Johnson I flew to New York each Wednesday evening to meet with our ad agency, the Froelich Co., on Thursdays, then flew back to Evansville Thursday evenings after our conferences. The Delta pilots chatted with us, their passengers most of the way to New York and back, pointed out the highlights of the scenery below. If we wished, once the seat-belt signs were off, we coach passengers could leave our seats and sit together on the big circular couch that stretched around the rear of the passenger compartment and swap stories with other frequent flyers From the cockpit: "Need anything from the stewardesses? Don't hesitate to ask." The stewardesses, sometimes wearing kid gloves, would see that we customers were fully served our food and drinks. It was like "When you fly with us, you're family." Thursday evenings, after our agency meet, our little group often finished the day with cocktails at the nearby Ambassador Hotel. I remember this one day. Henry Fonda, quite drunk, staggered by us as we entered the basement bar. We were having a great time and the time slipped by without my being aware. I had to grab my "Madison Avenue crash helmet," my new Knox felt hat that I had recently bought from Marshall Field, and scamper for a taxi to the airport.

On the Long Island Expressway, bumper-to-bumper 50 mph traffic, I tapped the driver on the shoulder and asked "I've really got to go to the bathroom. Could you turn off someplace?" To which he said something like "Man, can't you see this traffic? No way." A few minutes later I tapped him on the shoulder again and said, "If you can't find me a john, I'll have to pee in my hat." He didn't and I did. I threw my new Knox felt hat out the cab window onto the busy Long Island Expressway.

When I arrived home, Aggie, meeting me as usual at the airport, asked immediately "Where is your new Knox hat you just bought from Marshall Field?"

"Honey," I said, "let me tell you a story."

Entrepreneur in Action: Kon-Tiki Resorts
13 Years of Entrepreneurship, Fun and Profit on the Beach

At age 38 I wanted my own business. Mead Johnson had been very good to me for 13 years, but I felt that my business management skills were probably ready. Aggie and I gave a lot of thought to the question of where to start a new venture and raise two children. We narrowed it to Dallas, San Francisco, or Florida.

San Francisco was just "too far from family," so it lost out. We knew nothing about the great state of Texas, although as a boy, my folks had lived in San Antonio and McAllen for a year. But Sarasota had been home for five of my teen-age years. Florida in the thirties had been fun.

So Florida was it and Jacksonville specifically. "Jax" was nearing one million in population, At the crossroads of I-10 and I-95 it was a major distribution center. Everything entering or leaving Florida, including the CSX railroad, passed through Jax. It also appeared to be Florida's banking center. We bought a 5-bedroom, 3-bath, one-story home at the corner of Yacht Club and Pirate's Cove Roads.

In moving about the country, a wife's connections can be so important. Aggie was a Junior Leaguer, an ardent Red Cross worker, and joined in altar guild duties in Episcopal Churches in each city. In Albany and Evansville these had meant her instantaneous acceptance into groups of fine, intelligent young women.

The League and altar guild worked once again in Jacksonville. At the same time we were surprised by our next door neighbors. Our neighbors to the north, just across Yacht Club Road were Dr. Bill Croome and his wife Francis. I had known Bill from Chapel Hill days. He had the reputation in medical school of having a fabulous memory with instant recall. And across Pirates Cove Road to our east were Delbert and Fannie Conley. Aggie had gone to college with Fannie. We were lucky as could be once again. We knew we had bought on the right corner and lived there 45 years.

I became a manufacturer's representative. These guys, believe me, know exactly what's going on in whatever industry they work. They represent manufacturers who do not have sales forces or who need to have their sales force augmented in a specific area. Nobody knows more about the inner workings of any industry than the "reps." It's always a smart door to open to an industry that one would like to understand quickly.

In the 1960's "family camping" was coming into it’s own. With their tents, tent campers, pick-up truck campers, travel trailers and immense motor homes the size of Greyhound busses, families discovered a way *to improve their holiday situations.* Later these were called recreation vehicles or simply "RVs." Rather than paying $50 a night for a motel, they could take their RVs and spend only $10 a night in a national park or campground. A new industry sprang up almost overnight.

I located and brought together a line of auxiliary camping equipment: kerosene cook stoves, space heaters and lanterns from Germany, the Monolet, a fancy gold-colored bucket with a toilet seat and packs of chemicals. As a rep-distributor, I found a little old vacant house on the west side of Jax, hired a sturdy bookkeeper named Mildred Bishop, who agreed as her second job to ship the orders I sent her by phoning Railway Express to come pick up our stuff. My little enterprise was named Golden Crown Products.

And I hit the road. In a Chevrolet panel truck with shelving inside for my line of products, I traveled 60,000 miles a year covering every state east of the Mississippi except New England. I sold to hardware stores, trailer dealers, Western Auto stores and sporting goods stores who wanted to *improve their situations* by retailing camping-style products in a booming new industry. As I traveled and sent orders back to Mildred, I listened for opportunities *to improve my little company's situation.*

One of my customers, Charles McMahan, a travel-trailer dealer in Nashville, urged me to think in a *new but related direction.* "Bob," he would ask every time I visited him, "have you considered starting a campground? There's no place in Florida for all these families with all their new equipment to go to. There are a few state parks and the old mobile home parks, but mobile home parks are *definitely not the place to spend a Florida vacation.* I could send you a hundred new camping families every month. Think about it."

After a couple of years of 60,000 miles on the road, I took my friend Charles seriously and started my search for raw land. I covered every mile of Florida coast line, and there are about 900 miles of it. I wanted oceanfront. Florida, to people in Ohio, New York, and Tennessee meant the *beach, sand between their toes, and sunshine.* Most miles of Florida oceanfront were already built up with cities and hotels. *Then I found the answer.*

Thirteen miles south of St. Augustine, "the nation's oldest city," and only 50 miles from home in Jacksonville was *the spot.* There it was. It was pure virgin Florida oceanfront on a beautiful white sand beach. It covered 118 acres. *4.500 feet of virgin oceanfront by 800 feet of depth from Florida A-1-A, the state's most popular oceanfront highway.*

The vast acreage was owned by Kemmons Wilson of Memphis, founder and CEO of Holiday Inns of America. Kemmons had recently bought the tract at auction and had no immediate use for it, since he already had a Holiday Inn on the ocean two blocks north of this tract. He said he had been "passing by one day and had bought the tract as an investment."

So, off to Memphis where I found Kemmons Wilson and his attorney to be most sociable. Aggie's sister, Patty Dixon, lived in Memphis, so I sponged off sister Patty for a few days. Kemmons was interested in *improving his situation*. He wanted to enter the retirement home-nursing home business and already had a name for it: "Medicenters of America." He didn't want to sell his St. Augustine tract, but he would lease it to me. Leasing such a tract of land had several drawbacks, but I conferred with some Jacksonville businessmen, then our lawyer Mark Hulsey, and our accountants Dick Gray and Bill Kelly.

A Typical Conversation

It's surprising today, how new the Campground idea was then:

So now we have 118 acres on almost a mile of white sand Atlantic Ocean beach near the "nation's oldest city," itself a prime tourist attraction, and now we want this patch of sand dunes and arroyos to become a "campground/travel trailer park."

"A what? Like a mobile home park?"

"No, travel trailers are something new. They look like little mobile homes, but their new owners for sure don't want to drive a thousand miles from Illinois and spend their Florida vacation in a mobile home park. They've merely discovered a new way to avoid the high cost of hotels and motels."

"Oh, I see. But don't they use tents to camp in? When I was a boy scout, we camped out in tents."

"Yes, some families travel with tents. They're happy with a simple patch of sand where they can pitch their tent and enjoy your bathhouse."

"A bathhouse? Don't these little trailers have their own bathrooms?"

"Yes, but they're all scrunched up in about six square feet. In as little at 18 feet in length these travel trailers have little kitchens too and of course beds or bunks for each family member. But they all like the luxury of a full-sized shower when they park for the night, with plenty of hot water. Especially the women."

"So you just rent these trailers a little spot for the night?"

"For the night, a week, or months for some retirees. But each lot needs to have a hard, level area for the trailer to park so its floor doesn't slope, then each needs a hook-up for fresh water and electricity."

"Don't these trailers carry fresh water and have a battery like a car?"

"A matter of space again. The water supply is only a few gallons and they get their electrical power from the automobile that pulls them. Without an outside source of power overnight they would have a dead battery each morning. And each likes to have a nice sturdy picnic table on his little campsite."

"So they feel like they're camping out."

"That's it, and then we have the Florida sun, which along with the beach and the ocean is the big reason they have just driven a thousand miles down from Ohio. They need shade so the whole family doesn't get burned beet-red while sitting at their nice picnic table.

Each table needs an overhead shelter from the sun and rain. And then there must be hard roads throughout your big park so that cars and trailers don't get stuck up to their hubcaps in your soft sand. Not concrete roads; that's too citified, just hardened surfaces. And you must have a little building with a 'front desk' like a motel, to check your guests in and out. And a little general store complete with refrigeration, so they don't have to go all the way to Publix or Seven-Eleven every time they need eggs or a quart of milk.

"Sounds to me like you need a business plan."

"Is that like a marketing plan? I've been writing them for the last five years."

"Go to the library and tell the lady you want a book of business plans. She'll know what you want. Your lawyer, your accountant, your future shareholders don't want to hear about trailering and campgrounds. First thing they'll want to see is your business plan."

"And my banker will want that too?"

"Naw, all your banker wants to see is your personal financial statement."

"Oh, now I remember: *Research, manufacturing and marketing. All else is secondary."* Well, not quite. Funds *are* helpful.

We decided yes and leased 118 acres of prime, virgin Florida oceanfront. We would name it Kon-Tiki Family Campground, later to be shortened to Kon-Tiki Resorts. Aggie and I put up some of our Mead Johnson money and some of hers inherited from Uncle Rob. (You remember Uncle Rob who had sold to West Virginia drugstores on horseback.) Charles McMahan up in Nashville and his friend Lanny Hester became our early shareholders. In Jacksonville I brought in my neighbor, Clyde Higginbotham, a savvy life insurance agent, and then I found Jacksonville's greatest salesman.

His name was Harry Fromme, and until he died at 93 Harry was my best pal. Harry and his wife Peggy lived only six doors away, and Harry had traveled the world selling securities in Hong Kong, London and San Francisco. He added to our little shareholder group some true Jacksonville heavyweights such as Billy Arnold (who had built many of Jacksonville's office buildings), and twelve other top-tier local men with similar impressive business backgrounds.

On June 13, 1967, Kon-Tiki opened its doors with 110 campsites and with sturdy little bathhouses that were still short their toilet seats. Charles in Nashville sent us many of our first-night campers. We "cracked the nut" that first night and enjoyed a wonderful profit every month thereafter for 13 years.

Our big highway billboards on I-75, south of Valdosta, were placed there to catch and re-route camping families before they could continue south to Walt Disney World. Our big 18-foot signs shouted at them as they went by at 70 mph: "Camp On the Ocean Tonight at Kon-Tiki" That did it. Michigan camping families (and most others) decided they would do the Florida beach first. *They wanted the ocean! They could do Mickey Mouse the second week of their vacation.* They turned east off I-75 onto I-10 and pulled their trailers to St. Augustine Beach and the sunny, white-sand beaches of Kon-Tiki.

We made a few mistakes. We thought Kon-Tiki, being a family setting, should be alcohol free. That went out the rulebook in a hurry, but not before we had the guts to throw out the Rand-McNally salesman who was having a quiet beer at his campsite. Rand-McNally, you know, these are the people who publish maps, travel guides, and *directions to new campgrounds across America.* How dumb can one get?

We had a 20-foot high Easter Island figurehead built and put it on A-1-A. That became our trademark. Also a sign in good camping lingo: "Campers, you're here. *Hit Them Brakes*!" We heard from the literati about that.

Kids on the front porch of the store

Panoramic Arial Photo from Atlantic Ocean to Inter-coastal waterway

20-foot Kon-Tiki head at Entrance on Highway A1A

Family at their campsite table under their shelter

Teens running back to the beach

Two of Kon-Tiki's most popular postcards

Charles McMahan understood early on the appeal of the family campground. "When a family pulls their RV onto its little campsite, it's completely different from checking into a motel room where you never know who your neighbor across the hall might be. In the campground, the kids have been cooped up in the back seat of the family car for hundreds of boring miles. They burst from the car on the run. Within minutes they have met the other kids "across the street or next door" and are talking about tossing Frisbees down on the beach."

"Their parents, ready for a cold one, plunk themselves down at their picnic table and flip open a beer. "Next door" the family from Wisconsin has just pulled in. Only forty feet away from the other couple, the friendly talk begins.

It's the openness and the friendliness that puts all ages immediately at home. *No walls.* You never get that when you check in at a hotel. It's unlock the door and into the room. If you should happen to cross paths with your neighbor across the hall, it's 'Hi' and that's it. Camping and RVing satisfy the whole family."

Hundreds of guests became our friends as they returned year after year.

Fun!

A vacation destination enterprise is probably more fun than most. In the summer of 1990, taking a vacation myself, I discovered the particularly happy story of the Maine Coasting Schooner *Heritage.* Its co-captains, Douglas and Linda Lee of Rockland Maine did the entrepreneurial bit from original idea all the way to their places at the tiller of their completed 40-foot schooner. They had a plan.

First, many years before, the Lees went to Pratt Institute in Brooklyn and earned degrees in engineering. Then they returned home to Rockland, and with very little assistance over several years built a 40-foot schooner (no engine, so no engine room to take up space) with staterooms for 20 guests. When the boat was about ready, they began their advertising. Both Lees are personable, gracious hosts. In summers as they cast off from their Rockland dock for another week, Doug begins with his "sea stories." Guests soon chime in with more stories. Every week from June through September they sail the coastal islands of Maine and stuff their guests with lobster. An ideal fun enterprise, similar idea to an oceanfront campground.

Schooner" Heritage" out of Rockland Maine

Looking back over our records in 1980 we found that in 13 years *Kon-Tiki had played host to over one million families. We had been open night and day for thirteen straight years*. Like a hotel an RV park never closes its doors. Oh, I forgot. We did ask everyone to leave, then close for two nights during one September hurricane.

Thirteen non-stop years, a good reason for our physical facilities to become worn out. The sun, sand, and salt air our guests had come from Pennsylvania and New York to enjoy damaged our facilities considerably. Our electric hook-ups at the individual campsites were developing chronic shorts. The salt air had literally eaten up their copper and aluminum wiring. In our sewage treatment facility sand that had entered the system through the individual sewage hookups had eaten up the steel impellers that fed the raw sewage to the treatment vats. The plywood on the roofs at each campsite was separating and falling apart, worn out by the Florida sun.

To bring Kon-Tiki up to par once again would cost big bucks, *and we were on Kemmons Wilson's leased land.* At a meeting of our 22 shareholders, they were unanimous: Shut down. For each $10,000 they had invested they now received checks for $70,000. Our venture on the beach had performed very nicely.

From Entrepreneur to Free-Market
Research and Development

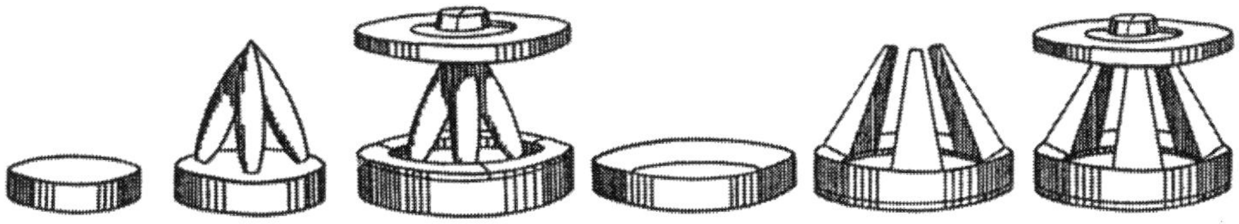

In 1980, I could make the case that Americans were growing weary with words. Words from TV, radio, internet and newspapers. Is there no relief from words spoken by reporters, by "news analysts," words from the Congress, words from people who *want a seat* in Congress, words from the White House?

After the sale of Kon-Tiki, my plan was to study "free-market economics." I wanted to approach that subject as an experienced marketing person, a former brand manager and recent entrepreneur. To define and clarify "Free-Market Economics" screamed "*Entrepreneurial Opportunity.*"

To me the "Free Market" was too important to be so abstract and so misunderstood by millions of Americans whose lives depended upon it. Not to mention the billions more around the globe who have never heard of it..

The subject had the earmarks of *"Public Ignorance in Extremis."* One example: two highly confusing everyday terms were "*conservative*" and "*liberal.*" Their meanings seemed completely different to different people and, even worse, their meanings seemed to have *reversed completely* over the last hundred years. And people using them thought they were communicating! Could our economists possibly clarify this for me? I began my study of subjects not included in my journalism curriculum at UNC-Chapel Hill.

I soon found that the "free-market" books I wanted most were not in my neighborhood library. Nor were they in our big downtown library. I learned that there were only three bookstores in America, in New York, New Orleans, and San Francisco, that stocked the books I most wanted. This was odd *but it confirmed strongly that I was onto a subject needing widespread clarification.* I began.

From the 15th century to the 19th, I learned, there was *the birth, the growth, and the maturation of a new discipline.* These new teachings were sometimes called *"economics" and some of the teachers "economists",* a new field of expertise with outstanding thinkers like these up through the 19th century:

Thomas Gresham 1519-1579	David Ricardo 1772-1873
Francis Hutchinson 1694-1746	George W. F. Hagel 1770-1831
Jean-Jacque Rousseau 1712-1778	John Stuart Mill 1806-1873
Adam Smith 1723-1790	Charles Darwin 1809-1882
David Hume 1711-1776	Friedrich Engels 1820-1895
Thomas Robert Malthus 1766-1834	Karl Marx 1818-1883

Coincidentally, both the USA itself and the "discipline of economics" had been *conceived* in the 15th century. Also coincidentally, both were *born two centuries later in the exact same year:* In 1776 the USA was born with Thomas Jefferson's "Declaration of Independence," and in 1776: "Economics" was born with Adam Smith's "*Wealth of Nations*." From that day, each developed and matured with distinguishing qualities that became steadily sharper. The United States began *to set itself apart* from other nations as it became recognized as the *new frontier of freedom.* Everyone in the 19th century, it seemed, wanted to live in the USA, and many millions booked passage to move here.

Then in the 20th century, ten modern economists I found were very interested in helping us set apart and understand the "free market." These persons made the subject understandable in their thoughtful and imaginative writings:

1881-1973	Ludwig von Mises	1912-2006	Milton Friedman
1894-1993	Henry Hazlitt	1922-2007	Hans Sennholz
1898-1983	Leonard E. Read	1925-2008	William F. Buckley, Jr.
1899-1992	Friedrich A. Hayek	1926-	Alan Greenspan
1905-1982	Ayn Rand	1936-	Walter Williams

Early in these years of research and development, I tried to hasten my R&D forward with three week-long summer seminars. First at the Foundation for Economic Education on the Hudson north of New York City; then at Hillsdale College in Hillsdale, Michigan; finally at Grove City College in western Pennsylvania. The same sharp, likable economist, Hans Sennholz, Chairman of the Economics Department at Grove City, was the director and key lecturer in each of these seminars. Sennholz was proud that he held one of only five PhD degrees granted by Ludwig von Mises. He taught us this: "In the private property order, all enterprises differ from all bureaus in that *every enterprise has a self-correcting, self-destructive mechanism. No bureaus have this mechanism."* Also at "FEE," I learned the first two steps in what I would define as the "Freedom to Choose."

They first two "characteristics" are: #1 - The purpose of all choices is to *improve the situation,* and #2 - Choices come in twos or more; a choice of one *is force.*

In the course of my reading, I discovered Milton Friedman's *Free to Choose,* where I learned that the theories of socialism, introduced by Franklin Roosevelt during the Great Depression of the 1930s *compounded* rather than *relieved* our nation's economic woes. Even more troublesome, FDR's wrong-headed "liberal" ideas continued to affect and disrupt our economy *from that time well into the 21st century.* Years later I had the opportunity to visit with Dr. Friedman at the Ponte Vedra Inn when he came to Jacksonville to receive an award from Jacksonville University.

The third most important economist in my education was Friedrich Hayek, who had been awarded a Nobel laureate two years before Milton Friedman's similar Nobel recognition. In 1974 I drove 900 miles from Florida to hear Hayek speak at the St. Louis Discussion Club at the old St. Louis Athletic Club, where he talked about "this little book," *The Road to Serfdom.* His most memorable and helpful statement: "*Liberty is a system under which all government action is guided by principles."* Two words: "system" and "principles" became the keys for development of my Philomod ® Model (model of a philosophy). *I felt that I was closing in on my answer, to improve the nation's situation which was a national shortage of free-market knowledge.*

The Philomod was to clarify TWO SYSTEMS: the Free-Market and the Anti-Market. This second phrase "Anti-Market," was my invented phrase to indicate *the directly opposing positions these two systems take in the real world.* Next SPECIFIC PRINCIPLES needed to be located, clarified, isolated, and grouped: *like principles with like principles, opposing principles grouped with other opposing principles.*

With these key ideas from Sennholz, Friedman, and Hayek (and the Declaration of Independence and Constitution), it would now be possible to construct, from New

England maple, a physical model, a device like a "classroom teaching aid" or a "lecture-circuit aid." *Similar principles* of thinking would be shaped alike. *Opposing principles* would somehow be shaped differently, so that opposing groups would be immediately recognized, when seen, then held in the hands, as being set apart and different from other groups.

Most important of all: the results of my research and development would be something *new, different, and quicker than simply another textbook. I felt I was closing in on the answer It would be a new, three-dimensional, visible, tangible sales tool.* I wished to present my "Free Market" subject not like an economics professor, (*for I was certainly not that)* but more like a sales manager talking with his group of salesmen: Not only imparting *knowledge of the product* but just as important: *how to sell the basic idea to others*.

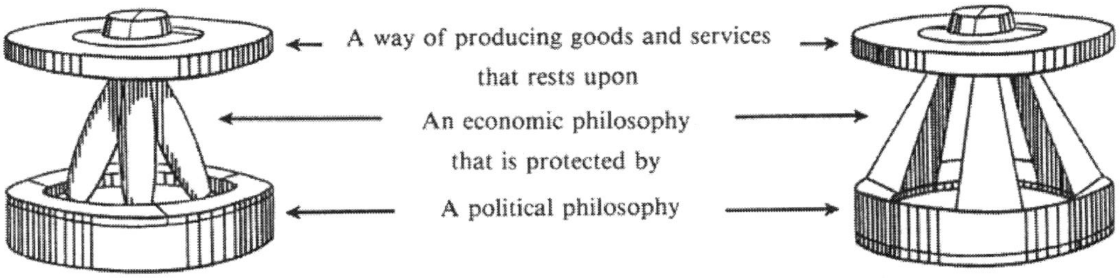

Five mentors upon whose ideas these structures are built:

Thomas Jefferson and James Madison.

The *political* concepts of our model are based upon the writings of Thomas Jefferson and James Madison. The first was the author of the Declaration of Independence. Madison has been called the "Father of the American Constitution."

Friedrich Hayek and Milton Friedman

The *economic* principles clarified by the model are based on the works of two Nobel Laureates in Economics: Friedrich Hayek, an Austrian, and Milton Friedman, an American. I have had the good fortune to personally shake the hands of both these men.

Peter F. Drucker

The *management* principles are based upon the works of our fifth mentor, Peter F. Drucker of the Claremont Graduate School in California. He has been called the father of modern American business management.

To Show Others the Way: The All-Language, Global Three-Dimensional Philomod ® Model

Welcome to structures made of hardwoods whose little shapes you can hold in your hands and *touch and feel* and *your eyes can see*. In your hands we offer you a relief from the confusing babble of worn-out words. These structures you can now hold are *building blocks.* Building blocks for old nations that should know better. But also building blocks for people who have lost hope, *who wish every day they too had a well-functioning nation*, and *for people who have not yet discovered that there is indeed hope.* In established nations there are *two Systems* and *fourteen Principles*.

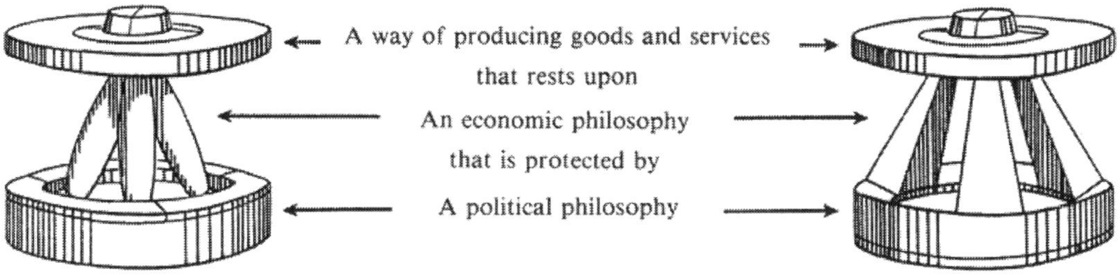

In This Chapter You Will Learn About:

A- The Organizational Structure

B - The Structure of Free Choice

C - The Economic Base of the Free Market

D - The Political Base of the Free Market

E - The Economic Base of the Anti-Market

Ask any college kid. Economics has the reputation of a "tough course." That means many pass over it for easier courses. That also means that "free-market economics" is either unavailable or avoided *for eight important years*, *from ages 13 to 21*. **No US high schools teach it. All State boards of education ignore it.** High school teachers as members of a teachers union deem it not in their best interest.

And yet, the subject, "Free-Market Economics" is the backbone of a free America. A subject students either can't have or they shun? American entrepreneurs stand in amazement. This is the spark that ignites our economy. Should anyone wonder why the United States in the 20th century slipped into its morass of socialist ways? *We became comfortable with "Ask the government to do it."*

Since the youngsters don't get or *choose not to get* "free market" education in school or college, *they hit the streets seeking their first job lacking basic, useful, day-to-day knowledge that would help them get the jobs they seek.* Their fathers may have taught their sons how to play catch and shoot baskets in the backyard, and their daughters to play the piano and go to dance school. Unfortunately, *because parents did not have the materials*, they could not favor their sons and daughters with a subject that could have been much more useful. The youngsters now tell us: *"Your information would have been so helpful. I wish I'd had it."* In 2011, these youngsters faced 35 weeks of unemployment. (Wall Street Journal 12/19/11) Job seekers outnumber job openings 6 to 1.

The parents had no tools to help their kids.

Now they have those answers.

When communicating intangibles like "free markets'" and "principles" it is so much quicker, more efficient and more thoughtful to use *three-dimensional* teaching aids. Think how many youngsters taking chemistry got the relationship between "molecules"

and "atoms" *in moments*, thanks to some *thoughtful, inventive, chemistry professor. You economics professors listening?*

The problem has been fixed through the introduction of a three dimensional, hand-held wooden teaching aid. The student is not forced to wrench free-market and business management "principles," made interesting by writers like Milton Friedman and Peter Drucker, from the pages of books. The Philomod model clarifies 14 principles through *their similar or differing shapes.* The student understands that a certain group of four principles (pieces or shapes) assure a nation a "Free-Market philosophy. "From other shapes he can hold, he *sees and feels* their difference. The *others* build an "Anti-Market philosophy" or bureaucracy. *The student's "free enterprise" free-market education is underway.*

Peter Drucker, father of "Management Principles and Practices" in the 20th century, wrote: "The work of the world is done through organizations." With some study of this commandment, we learned that, not only do organizations do all the work of the world, *every one of them can be divided into the same five parts, or pieces, or principles.*

A The Organizational Structure

Pieces (7) **Creativity**
(8) **Management**
(9) **People Resources**
(10) **Property Resources**
(11) **Products and Services**

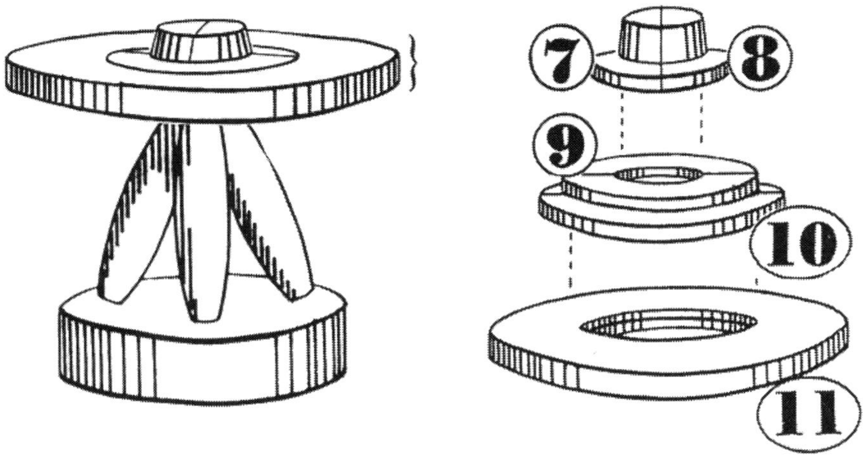

In the Philomod Model, every organization is shaped like a wagon wheel with a hub. Our hub on all Philomod models, is divided into two halves. The first half is where almost every organizational action in the world begins. It is Piece 7: "CREATIVITY and INNOVATION." That is the first spark of a new idea that has someone excited. It is the pre-conception, probably not yet fully formed in the mind. *It's an idea that appears worth developing*. Creativity and imagination is where the fun starts! Inside your brain, this is what can happen *in your right lobe.*

A lot is known about creativity. Here are a few tips. Creative minds and creativity are stimulated by three factors:

1 - **Input**. The mind is fed an incredibly broad mixture of hard facts, soft

impressions, old wives' tales and dogma -- millions of bits of general stimuli. The mind also needs to be fed selective high-quality information relating to the *specific interests of the individual and the challenges at hand.*

2 - **Respite**. The subconscious mind is quite disorderly, working best when it is allowed to develop ideas at its own pace. Ideas form continuously even when ignored by the conscious mind. To try to rush their formation usually accomplishes little. In their own time they assume a usable shape and are then recognized-- *sometimes quite suddenly* -- by the conscious mind. Eureka!!

3 - **Motivation**. Individuals are motivated best according to their individual preferences. Rewards serve as psychological stimuli and may be either material or non-material. Skilled managers know their people and know which rewards motivate different personalities. New small enterprises are frequently more creative than large organizations and are invariably more so than anti-market bureaus. Just as there are *stimulators*, there are *inhibitors* of creativity, for example:

Lack of input or the wrong input

Fear of failure or ridicule

Restrictions upon rewards

Regimentation, too many rules

Not enough time to think.

Piece 8, "MANAGEMENT." Now we switch from the right lobe of your brain to the left lobe, your "logic" lobe. Management guides the organization in turning ideas into marketable goods and services. The entrepreneurial task is to define the market and, as the glove is made to fit the hand, to mold a product or service to fit.

Management must balance the resources available to deliver a product or service that represents good value at a reasonable price and is profitable to the organization. Management does its job through *planning, organizing and controlling.*

1 - Planning. The emerging enterprise starts with a written business plan - an absolute necessity if the organization is to attract venture capital. It defines the market need and tells why its product idea fills that need; sets objectives, priorities, and a timetable; projects income, costs, and capital required; and provides resumes of the founder and his associates.

2 - Organizing. Setting up a structure; seeing that the key marketing, manufacturing, and financial functions are covered and responsibilities understood; that legal requirements are met; that suitable space, equipment and working capital are obtained.

3 - Controlling. Guiding the organization; seeing that each person in the organization is carrying out his part of the plan so that objectives are met; and seeing that - within an agreed period of time - the enterprise becomes profitable.

Pieces 7 and 8 interact with one another like the two halves of the human brain. Piece 7 *forms*. Piece 8 *transforms*. Piece 7 is the *originator*. Piece 8 is the *implementor*. When the two pieces, #7 and #8 are placed together in our model, we call them the **ENTREPRENEURIAL HUB.**

When we try to place Pieces 7 and 8 at the top of the structure, they fall apart. *They won't stay there.* Needed next is the *Resources Ring*. This ring, also divided into halves, is made up of two types of resources: Piece 9 *People Resources* and Piece 10 *Property Resources*.

People Resources, Piece 9. These give the organization its unique personality and set it apart from others. This blend is the total of the organization's aptitudes, interests, abilities, objectives, motivations, self-discipline, and appearance. Here we meet the employees who contribute to the creativity and innovation of Piece 7, but mainly with their computers in the offices and their equipment on the factory floor, produce the finished product: Piece 11.

Property Resources, Piece 10. These are the capital resources and the raw materials - "things" as differentiated from "people." Organizations can own things like patents, land, buildings, computers, and equipment. But in a free-market society, organizations cannot own people. Note again how our model is constructed. Even now, with the Resources Ring in place, neatly fitted around the Entrepreneurial Hub, *the structure still will not hold together.*

End Products and Services, Piece 11, *is the reason for the organization's existence.* It's the end result of the Original idea - Piece 7. Piece 11 is the product that successfully matches the *needs, wants, or preferences of the market, that improves the situation.* The marketable *product* rests upon the *resources ring*, which rests upon the *entrepreneurial hub*, which is balanced atop the *Freepod.* Each piece, 7 through 11, is completely dependent upon all the others.

Hans Sennholz taught us this: *"All enterprises are designed with a Self-Correcting, Self-Destructive Mechanism: Without The Successful Product, They collapse and die."* This means the enterprise, through its products, people, and services must ***Improve the Situation*** *in some way in the eyes of its customers.* ***This alone is the basis of all success or failure of enterprise. Remember this above all else, because this is the magic key of the philosophy called Capitalism.*** This explains the two color shots of our Philomod.

On the Front Cover of This Book:

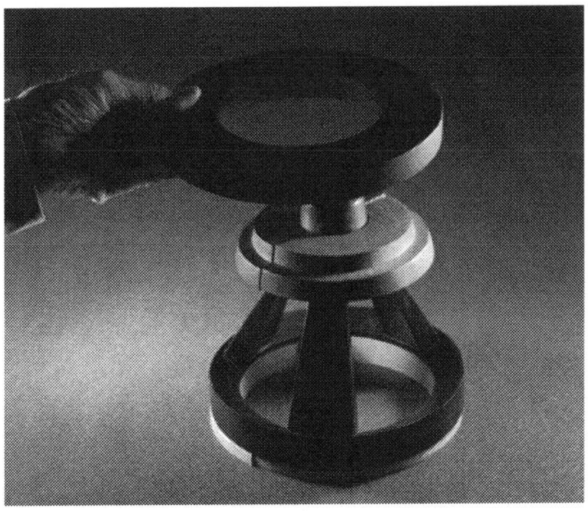

Why Capitalism Works... **...Why Socialism Does Not**

This brings us to the most important piece or principle in the Philomod Model.

B The Structure of Free Choice

Piece ① Your Freedom To Choose

First, each of us is surrounded by choices.

Some we face are very large, such as choosing how we will earn our livings, whom we will marry, and where we will live. *We live with the outcomes of these three choices 24 hours a day, seven days a week, year after year.*

Other big choices are:

1 - The kind of person we want to be

2 - How we use our time

3 - How we utilize our natural talents

4 - How we care for our bodies

5 - Our moral and religious values

Second, there is the Freedom to Choose

We will portray freedom to choose as a large disk on which we can walk, run, work or relax. *If we are Americans,* this disk was given to us at birth.

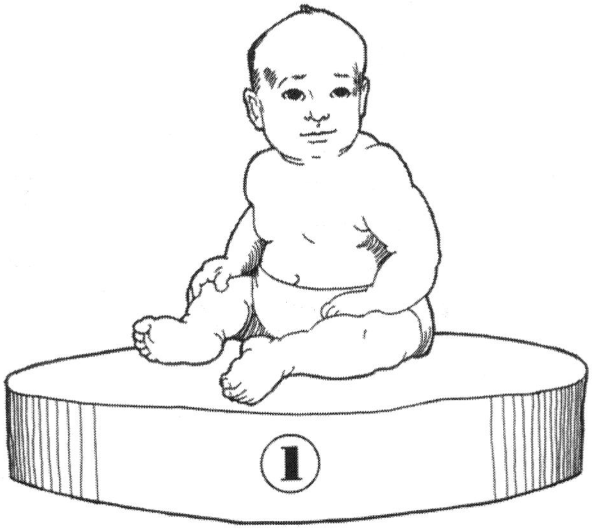

It is your and yours alone. You may use this disk well or poorly, but you cannot shake it. It is yours for life.

In the Philomod Model, we call this Freedom-to-Choose disk Piece 1.

Next, imagine this disk sliced into two thinner disks. One of these thinner disks is called the Characteristics of Choice. The Characteristics of Choice disk is composed of ten wedges. The other disk is the Choosing Process disk and is composed of eight wedges. The Characteristics of Choice disk has ten.

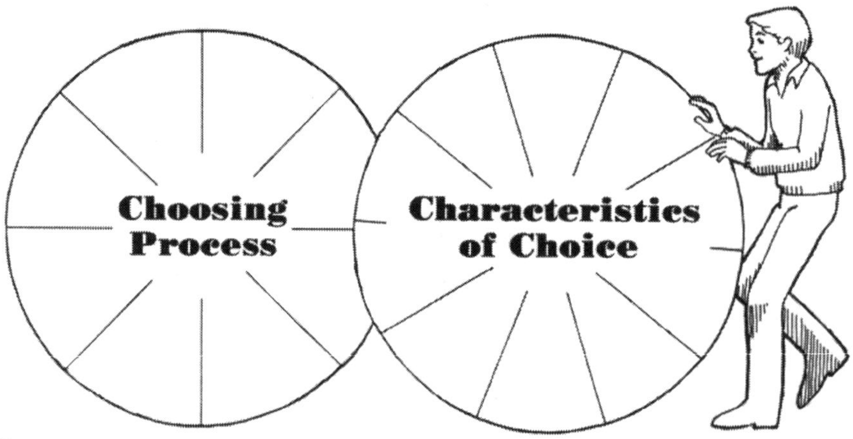

Imagine walking around on top of your disk, stepping from one wedge-shape to next. You will always end up back at your starting point. *Thus you are in a position to start again, just in case you feel you have not improved your situation (the purpose of all choices).*

So each of us, as Americans, is 1) surrounded by choices, 2) each of us has a lifetime base called the freedom-to-choose. And this Freedom-to-Choose disk is made up of ten Characteristics of Choice and eight steps or phases in the Choosing Process.

The Ten Characteristics of Choice ... The "CC's"

These ten principles are based upon reason. Thomas Jefferson might have called them "self-evident truths."

CC-1 Choices have a common purpose: to improve the situation.

CC-2 Choices come in two's or more; a choice of one is force.

CC-3 To achieve the best outcomes, include the best input.

CC-4 Every choice has an "opportunity cost" or trade off.

CC-5 Choices are subjective value preferences.

CC-6 Choices are made with limited time and information.

CC-7 Choices involve unknowns, uncertainties, and risks.

CC-8 Choices have primary and secondary consequences.

CC-9 We alone are responsible for our choices.

CC-10 The weightier the decision, the more difficult to change.

The Eight Phases of the Choosing Process...The "CP's"

Some modern managers have suggested that major decisions often employ a process that goes through eight phases:

CP-1 Awareness... A feeling of uneasiness

CP-2 Definition... Find the problem and define it

CP-3 Analysis... Consider the characteristics, the CC's

CP-4 Collection... Collect and create alternative solutions

CP-5 Decision... Decide on the best solution

CP-6 Communication... Tell those who need to know

CP-7 Action... Make the change decided upon

CP-8 Evaluation... Has the situation actually improved?

We'll refer to these CC's and CP's frequently. They're basics. These are the practical ways most of us can get a lot more mileage out of the choices that surround us. Helpful in life's everyday struggles, useful for an entire lifetime.

All 10 Characteristics and Eight Phases are permanently saved for you on the Philomod product label, attached to the bottom of every Piece No. 1

This is worth remembering:

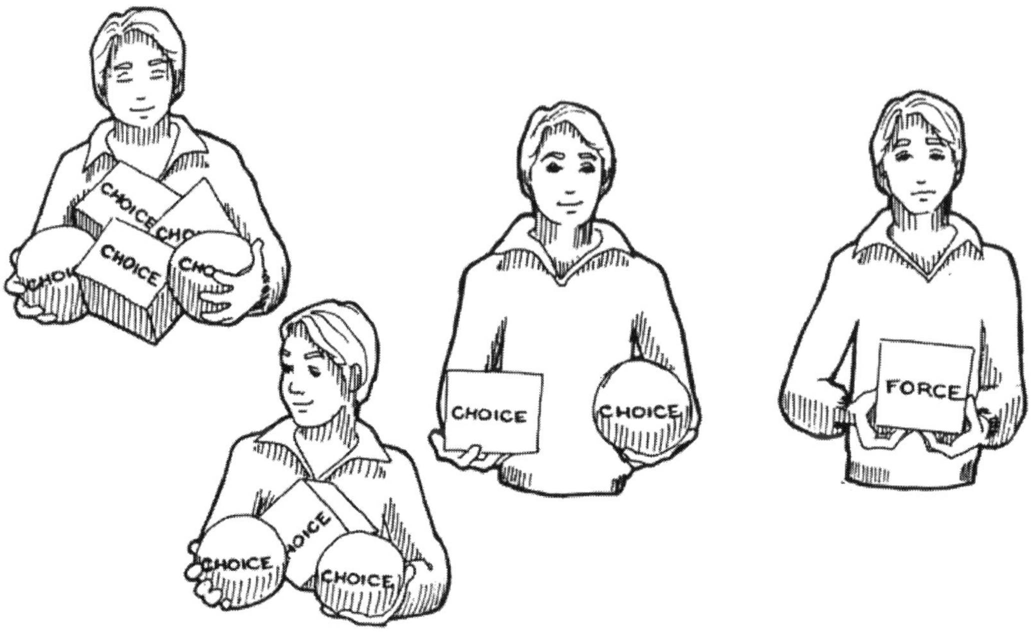

That your life might be more full of confidence:

C - The Economic Base of the Free Market

Pieces ② Freedom to Own
③ Freedom to Exchange
④ Freedom to Fund

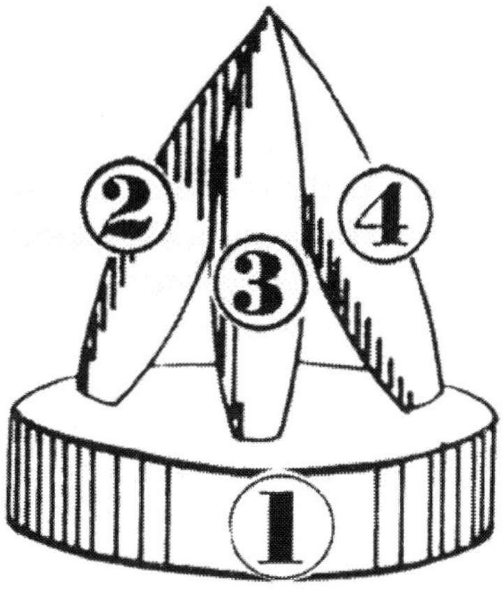

These three round legs are based upon the disk, Piece 1, and comprise Philomod® Institute's "Freepod."

Piece 2: Freedom to Own represents the right of property ownership in the free society. Not only can we own property, we are also free to own private *productive* property, properties that are used to produce goods and services. These organizations are owned by individual persons or groups of individuals. They are not owned by the government or any of its agencies.

Note: the freedom to own includes the freedom not to own, if that is our choice. Piece 2 represents only voluntary ownership. The properties that each of us owns are (1) ourselves, (2) our productivity, and (3) our correctly acquired property, as the original claimant to un-owned property-- such as finding a shell on the beach-- or as the secondary claimant through the freedom to exchange. Example: buying the shell from its owner for a dime.

Piece 3 :Freedom to Exchange is the second round leg. It was necessary to tie down *ownership* concepts before we explore *exchange* concepts, because we can exchange or trade only what we own. Just as being free to choose is a necessary precondition to our being free to own, being free to own is necessary precondition to our being free to exchange.

Before going further, we should define two terms, the economic *problem* and the economic *solution*. Simply stated, the economic problem is *scarcity* and the economic solution is *productivity*. Basic points in the philosophy of capitalism When we are young it seems that almost all of us are short on worldly goods. We want to improve our situation (CC-1), to relieve the scarcities we face. What do we do? We exchange what we have-- and which we value (CC-5)-- for something the other fellow owns (which we value even more). What we own is our personal productivity. We want to exchange our ability and willingness to produce for the other fellow's property (his money).

We talk about "finding a job." The employer talks about "finding someone who will do the job." We go to the store and "buy" an item we want. The store "sells" it to us. Yet all these phrases are really another way of describing an exchange. If the exchange does not make both of us happier, it doesn't take place.

When the exchange does take place, each has *improved his situation* as he sees it at the time (CC-l). Free exchange in a competitive market means anyone can enter and anyone can play. Free choice always offers us a choice of two or more products or services, because a choice of one is not a choice; it's force (CC-2). *Competition offers choices.*

Piece 4: Freedom to Fund is the third round leg in the Freepod. This principle lets us organize our own property and the property of others (investors) who wish to participate voluntarily in risk taking, to fund a productive enterprise in the *hope of a reward*, again simply trying to *improve the situation*.

Piece 4 tells us that we support productive organizations freely and voluntarily in two ways: First we may support an organization in its inception (when it may be nothing more than an idea) with our actions and/or our property(capital). We invest in it voluntarily-- even though there are unknowns, uncertainties and risks (CC-7) -- in the belief there will be a reward. The reward we seek may be any material or psychic return that satisfies our individual value preferences (CC-5).

Second, we help sustain an organization once it is underway. As an organization produces competitive goods and services, it attracts customers who purchase them. We thereby help sustain an organization, not with the assurance of profit, but with the *opportunity* for profit through sound investment.

In sum: Free organizations are funded at their inception by capital (property). Once their revenues exceed their costs, once they have shown that they *improve the situation* they are funded by the profit they earn through free exchange.

Not all free-market organizations are enterprises, intended for profit. Churches and certain types of schools and universities, for example, are also based upon the principles of the Freepod -- voluntarily *owned*, in a voluntary *exchange* of their services, are voluntarily *funded.* While such organizations do not strive to "earn a profit," they too will fail if their costs are not covered by their incomes. This brings us to the subject of The Political Base of the Free Market.

D - The Political Base of the Free Market

Pieces 5 Centralized Governmental Power
⑥ Limitation and Dispersion Of Governmental Power
① Freedom To Choose

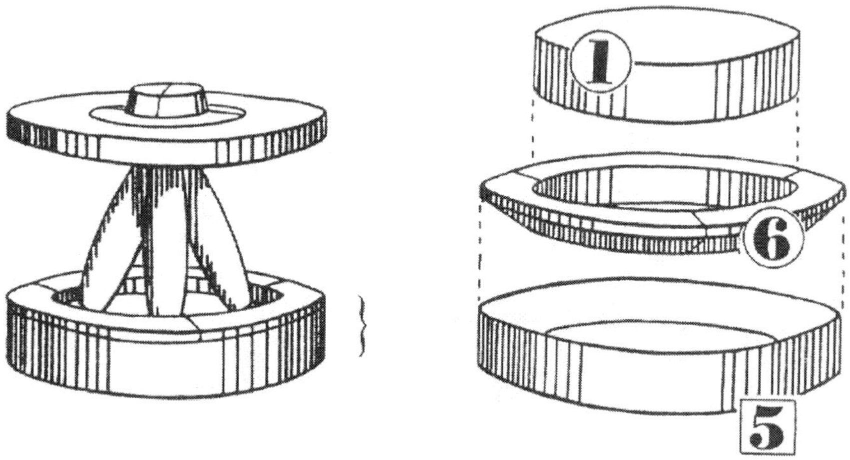

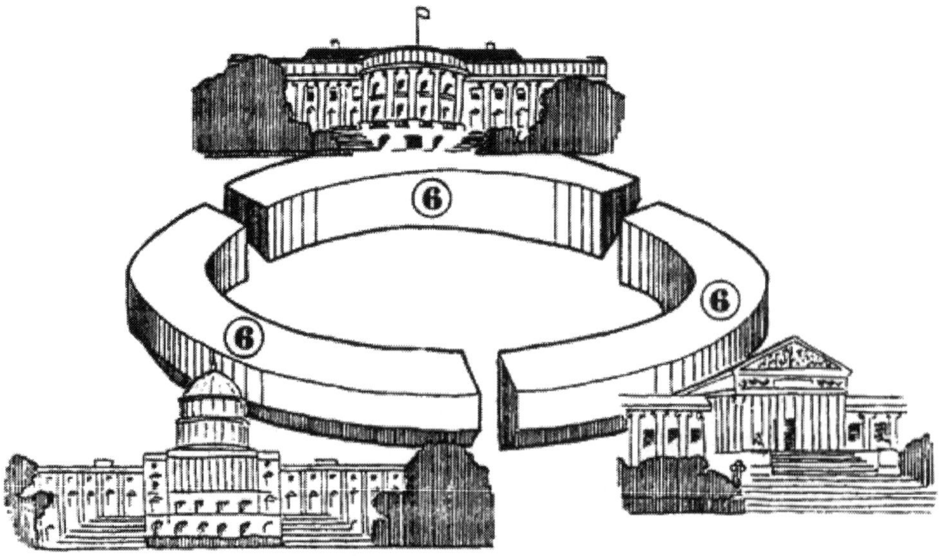

To this point all pieces in our substructures have been identified by numbers in circles. These pieces represent elements in the free market and are associated with *round* legs in the model. Now we will introduce four *square-shaped* pieces identified by numbers in squares, to indicate that they are anti-market forces. Pieces 5 and 6 are rings to protect Piece 1, your freedom to choose. They represent governmental principles and policies. The Purpose of Government is to Protect...Freedom of Choice

Patrick Henry: "The Constitution is not an instrument for the government to restrain the people. It is an instrument for the people to restrain the government, lest it dominate our lives and interests."

Thomas Paine: "It is the duty of the patriot to protect his country from his government."

Piece 5 *Centralized Governmental Power*, such as the Department of Defense and the Department of State. The Defense Secretary can exert force through men and arms. The Secretary of State exerts power through diplomatic persuasion.

"But hold on there," said the Founding Fathers as they were writing the Constitution, "what will protect us from centralized power itself?" Thus they gave birth to those unique ideas which are the basis for the three parts that form Piece 6.

Piece 6 *Decentralization and Limitation of Power*, as called for in the Constitution, Piece 6, for that reason, is actually composed of *three different pieces*, each a third of a circle, into *three functional branches*: the executive, the legislative, and the judicial. Also it represents *decentralization by three strata and geography-- federal government, state government, and the people.* This is clarified in Amendment X in the Bill of Rights "The powers not delegated to United States by the Constitution, nor prohibited by it to the states, *are reserved to the States respectively, or to the people."* The other third to limit governmental power is "checks and balances." The Founding Fathers created a system of these checks and balances: The House must originate all money bills, subject to the review of the Senate and the veto of the President. The Senate must approve the President's appointments to the cabinet. The President's appointment of Supreme Court justices must be approved by the Senate. There are many more. The freedom to choose is best protected by a delicate balance of *force* and *dispersion of force.* Simply stated in the "shorthand" of the Philomod model:

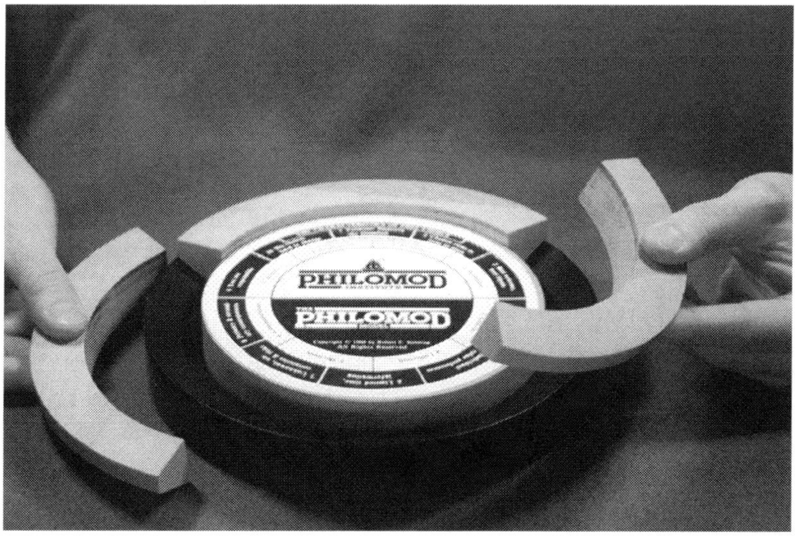

The purpose of Piece 5 is to protect Piece 1. But what is to protect 1 from 5? That is the role of Piece 6-- to check and restrain Piece 5! Three protections have been accomplished: *Limitation, Dispersion, and Decentralization of Power. Which is on top, Piece 6 or Piece 5? Here lies substantial danger. When Piece 6 is on top of Piece 5,* the configuration favors the protection and continuation of freedom and free-market organizations. Piece 1, Freedom to Choose, can be in the middle to support the *three round legs* and the *free market* organization atop them.

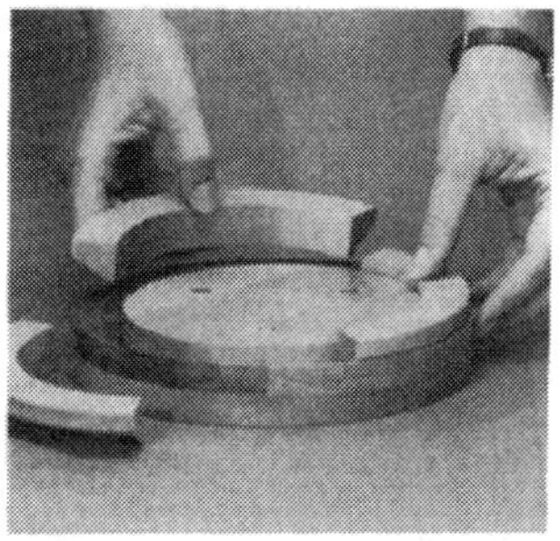

But *when Piece 5 is on top*, then the *tapered ring is wide open to serve as the support for* the *three square legs* and the anti-market organization atop them. Next you will be introduced to Pieces 12, 13, and 14...*Force.*

A Check to Political Power Rather Than a Reinforcement

Milton Friedman identified another form of decentralization of power. Although our Founding Fathers certainly realized this, they did not define it as explicitly as Friedman: "*By removing the organization of economic activity from the control of political authority, the market eliminates the source of coercive power. It enables economic strength to be a check to political power rather than a reinforcement.*"

E - The Economic Base of the Anti-Market

Pieces
- **12** **Public Ownership**
- **13** **Controlled Exchange**
- **14** **Mandatory Funding**

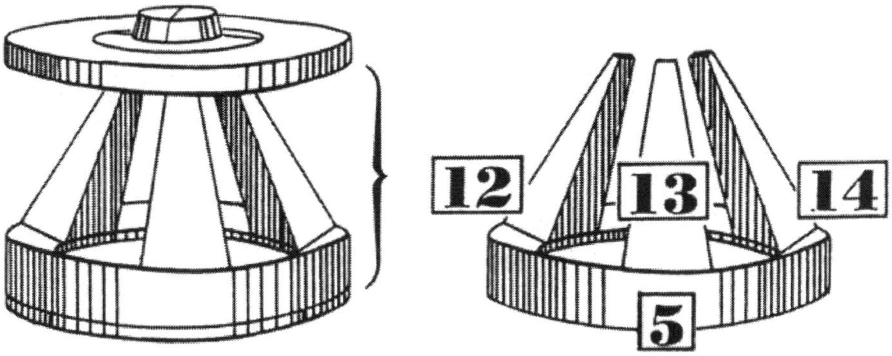

"*Government is not reason, it is not eloquence -- it is force! Like fire it is a dangerous servant and a fearful master; never for a moment should it be left to irresponsible action.*" - George Washington

Nobel economist Friedrich Hayek suggested: "We can better understand *our own principles*, if we study those *that oppose them*."

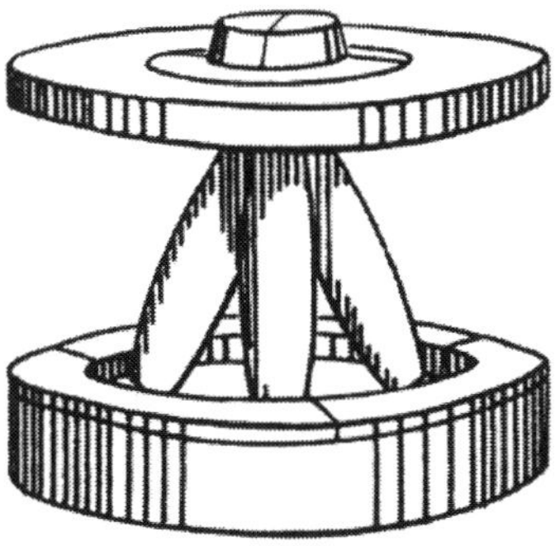

THIS A MODEL OF:

← An operating PRIVATE organization

based upon

← An *economic* philosophy of FREE markets

protected by

← A *political* policy of LIMITED governmental power

We have completed our look at an operating *private* organization--the enterprise.

Now we will look at the opposing philosophy, an operating public organization -- based upon an economic philosophy of *controlled markets,* and protected by a *political policy of unlimited governmental power.*

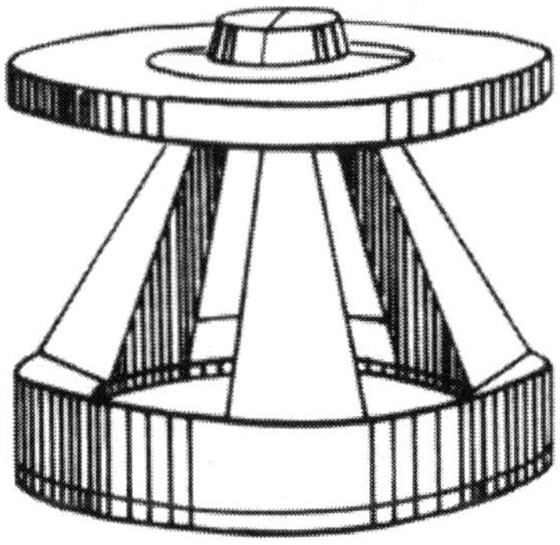

THIS IS A MODEL OF:

An operating PUBLIC organization

based upon

An *economic* philosophy of CONTROLLED markets

protected by

A *political* policy of UNLIMITED governmental power

Now we have an organization represented again by the five piece wagon wheel shape at the top. (All organizations, remember, are made up of the same five principles.) But this organization is based upon *three-square legs. This organization is called a Bureau,* not an enterprise.

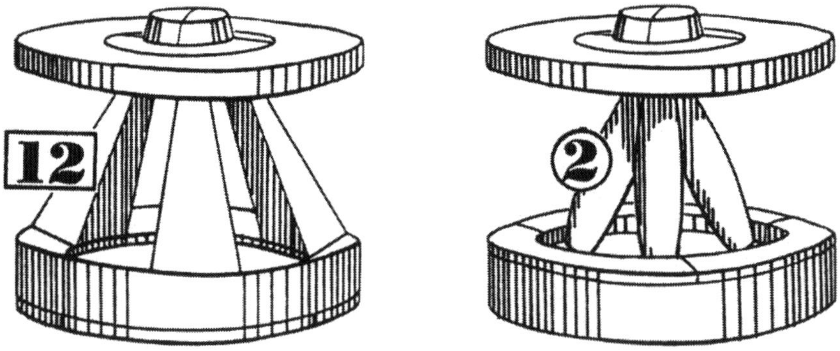

Piece 12. Governmental Ownership of Productive Property

This is the antithesis of Piece 2, Private Ownership. Basic to the concept of the anti-market is governmental ownership of productive organizations. Examples are the Tennessee Valley Authority, which during the depression went into competition with Duke Power; Amtrak, which competes with CSX Rail, Norfolk Southern, and other privately owned railway companies. Who is the *largest printer* in the United States? The *largest producer of motion pictures*? Our Federal Government.

How do governments come to own productive properties?

1 - They acquire them as the original claimant.

2 - They purchase them as the secondary claimant with funds obtained through (a) borrowing -- the sale of bonds, (b) taxation, or (c) inflation of the currency.

3 - They take title through legislation (condemnation of private property).

4 - They simply take them through military action.

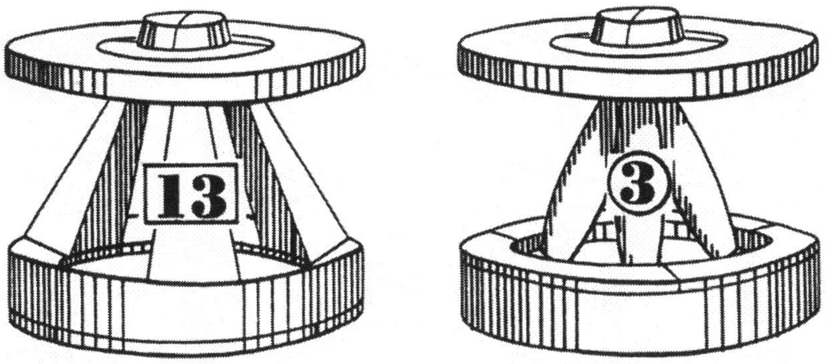

Piece 13: *Controlled Markets, Restricted Exchange.* This is the antithesis of Piece 3, Freedom of Exchange. Anti-market organizations interfere in our free-market choosing processes in at least three ways:

1 - They control market PRICES

2 - They control market PRODUCTS

3 - They limit market ENTRY

Control of Market Prices. When the anti-market interferes with the free market through price, interferences cause either shortages or surpluses. If the AM sets a price too high, the FM produces too much. If the AM sets the price too low, the FM produces too little. The Labor Department administers the minimum wage, resulting in a price too high for many small entrepreneurs.

The result: unemployment among young people. The Agriculture Department sets artificially high prices on peanuts. Many farmers, who are of course entrepreneurs, choose to plant peanuts instead of some other crop.

Control of Market Products. The Federal Reserve and the Congress have almost complete control over monetary and fiscal policy. Through the expansion of credit they mislead the businessman and throw the marketplace into confusion. Secondary consequences (CC-8) are at work. AM organizations are notorious for the ignorance, disregard, and oversight of secondary consequences. As the AM disrupts the FM in millions of ways each day, it interferes with prices. Who pays? The consumer of course. Pharmaceutical manufacturers know all about the risks, unknowns, and uncertainties (CC-7) of marketing new drugs.

The Food & Drug Administration may sit on new life-saving drugs for years before granting approval. (Lessons learned in the pharmaceutical industry: At Mead Johnson in the 1950's our pharmaceutical company employed *only one in-house attorney*. Today, to cope with FDA requirements, one of the major pharmaceutical manufacturers *must employ 200 in-house attorneys*. Wonder why your drugs cost so much? A major reason: the costs of dealing with the government.

Want to build a golf course? Amelia Island Plantation north of Jacksonville had to get approvals from *forty-one different* federal, state, and local bureaus; and it *took three years*, and cost $2 million, *just to get the okays before construction could even begin. Millions of entrepreneurs contend with such regulations daily. Not fun.*

Limitations on Market Entry. These treat your way of earning a living as a privilege. If you want to drive a cab in New York City, first you'll need to buy a $50,000 "medallion." If you want to be a plumber, electrician, beautician, or barber, first you must obtain an occupational license. *You must obtain a license to enter you own profession!* You'd like to peddle tickets in the numbers game? You'll be arrested. *And yet 39 states now have gambling.*

One standard measurement of anti-market growth is the number of pages in each year's Federal Register. The next chapter in this book may shock you!

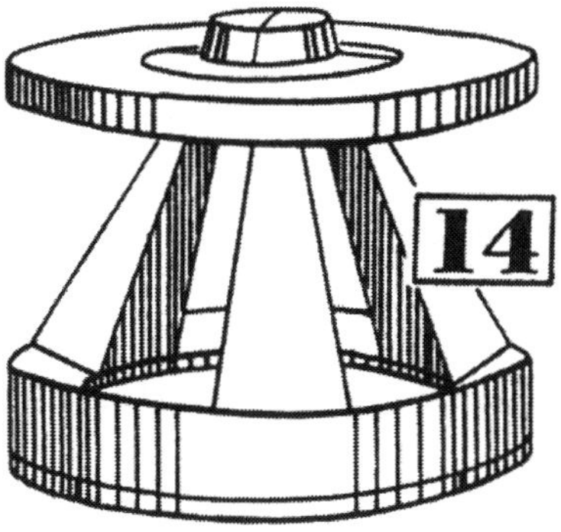

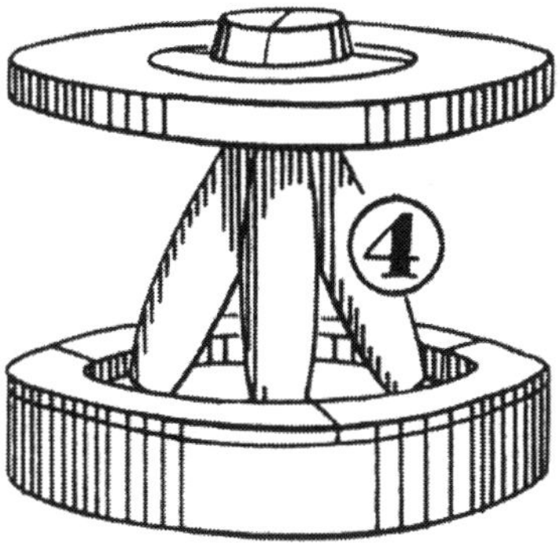

Piece 14 Mandatory Funding, Taxation and Inflation

This is the antithesis of Piece 4, Freedom to Fund (or not to). The third square leg of the anti-market tripod is involuntary or forced funding. *The Anti-Market cannot create wealth. It can only take wealth from individuals and free-market organizations, whether they improve the situations of those individuals and organizations or not.*

Every choice has a cost (CC-4). The cost to the FM is that the AM forcefully diverts capital resources, natural resources, and human resources for its own purposes, thus withholding from -- and weakening-- the free market.

The Free-Market (FM) Principles Group...

① Freedom to Choose
② Freedom to Own
③ Freedom to Exchange
④ Freedom to Fund

...Surrounds Us With Free Choices.

The Anti-Market (AM) Ideologies Group...

[5] Centralized Governmental Power
[12] Governmental Ownership of Property
[13] Controlled Markets
[14] Mandatory Funding

...Can Block Us From Our Choices.

Because governments rarely live within their incomes, and because people will only stand for so much taxation, governments inflate their currencies. Governments are strangely selective in what and how quickly they learn. Some things, like free-market concepts, they avoid learning. But other things-- such as how to inflate the currency-- they all learn.

In the mid 1960s, all the silver disappeared from US quarters, half dollars and silver dollars. Sterling silver in 2011 is expensive: $30 an ounce. Sterling silver was replaced with a pot metal, *then coated over with silver.* Even pennies were inflated.

Copper is also *expensive*, so it was replaced with zinc, cheap as dirt, *then coated over with copper.*

The organizations that do not self-destruct. Remember *"every enterprise has a built-in self-correcting, self-destructive mechanism?"* When we placed the organization representing an enterprise atop the three round legs representing our free-market principles, *then removed the successful end-product or service, the organization collapsed! Because it did not produce a product that its customers thought improved their situations, meaning a profitable product, it went bankrupt.*

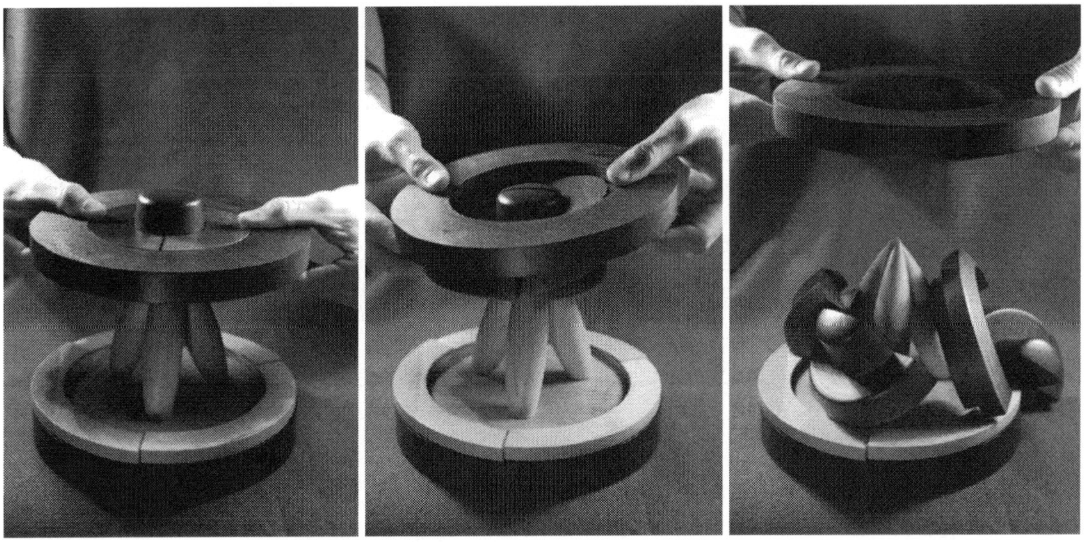

Now let's see what happens when we remove Piece 11, the end-product or service ring from the *anti-market bureaucratic structure.*

This structure does not collapse. It lives on. There it stands, a structure with no purpose. Whatever product or service this organization was supposed to produce either failed or has long since been forgotten. Piece 5, Centralized Governmental Power will support this meaningless structure, feeding it our taxpayer funds through Piece 14 forever.

Unfortunately, TIME FAVORS ANTI-MARKET ORGANIZATIONS. Here are two facts you should know about our free-market organizations in the United States:

1 - Of all the new enterprises that are formed each year in the US, **93** percent will be broke and out of business *within three years.*

2 - Of the millions of existing organizations in the United States, from giant Exxon-Mobil down to Mama's Pizza Parlor, *their average age is only 15 years.*

This helps explain our twentieth century tragedy, our 100 trillion dollar unfunded debt that special "super committees" of Congress must try to resolve.

Enterprises are Mortal: They are born, They live for a few years, or as long as they improve the situation and they die. But bureaus that are given a birth can live forever whether they improve the Situation or not, they are immortal. You now see why the free –market to anti-market Ratio always runs against enterprise and freedom of choice.

What is the Lesson?

This is the major message of the Philomod Model. If free-market organizations self-destruct when they no longer produce an end-product consumers believe improves their situation, and, if anti-market bureaus do not, even though they have not significantly improved the situation, the ratio of AM and FM organizations must shift, causing anti-market communities to grow. A relatively static-sized or slow-growing free-market community may then be expected to support a growing anti-market community of organizations. In the United States, but more evident today in the old European nations, this shift has brought about very painful circumstances, even riots in the streets. Capitalism usually works well because of its self-cleansing, self-destructive mechanisms. Socialism, lacking these self-cleansing mechanisms, grows too large, becomes a burden and eventually must fail.

Stop now asking the government to improve your situation. As an American you yourself should tackle those problem situations. If you feel some situation should be improved... if possible, you improve it. You. First, you will certainly do it BETTER than the government. Second, you will enjoy a wonderful sense of satisfaction.

Perhaps you are seeking the formation of a new bureau and don't realize it. Now you know three basic questions to ask:

1 - May I "Own" this organization or an organization like it? If it will be another bureau, the answer is No.

2 - May I "Compete" with this organization? If it will be another bureau, the answer is No.

3 - Must I "Fund" this organization, whether it improves the situation or not? If it is another bureau, that answer is: Yes you must.

Parents Can Now Step In.

Parents, who might have expected schools to teach freedom principles, can now fill that deadly void. Buy, borrow or steal a Philomod Model to clarify free-market principles for your children. Now *You Have the Tools,* to do the job your high schools and colleges did not do, and to do it even better.

Finally, You Can Show Others the Way...

The situation has now been made clear. The truth that makes you free: *Free Enterprise, Freedom Itself, is no longer a phantom cloud, dominated by complex words floating about in the fog.*

"Freedom" now has a Structure... a visible, tangible, three-dimensional structure, with a base named "Freedom to Choose," and on that base three legs that define Three Actions named "Freedom to Own, Freedom to Trade, and Freedom to Fund. (or not to)"

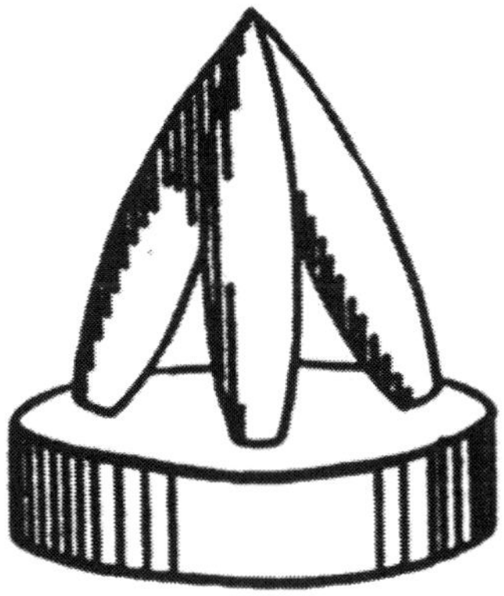

Atop these four-piece structures, there are five-piece Organizations called Enterprises. You can now understand why Enterprises are the Only True Engine of Prosperity and Wealth.

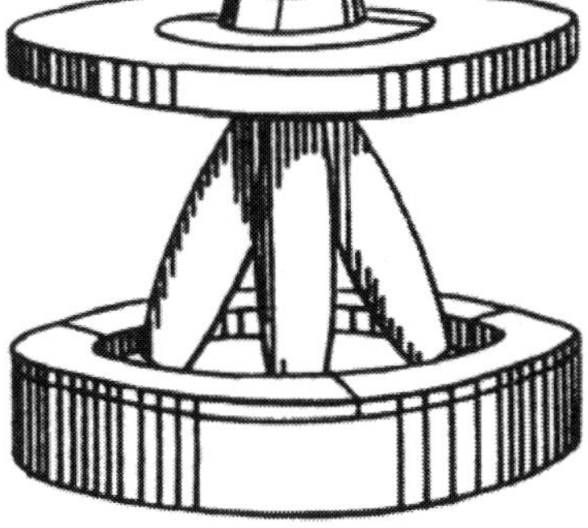

Never be *misled* by *non-productive substitute organizations.*

Liberty is a system under which all government action is guided by principles
Friedrich A. Hayek, Nobel Laureate, 1974

Overview of the Philomod Model

There Are Two Systems

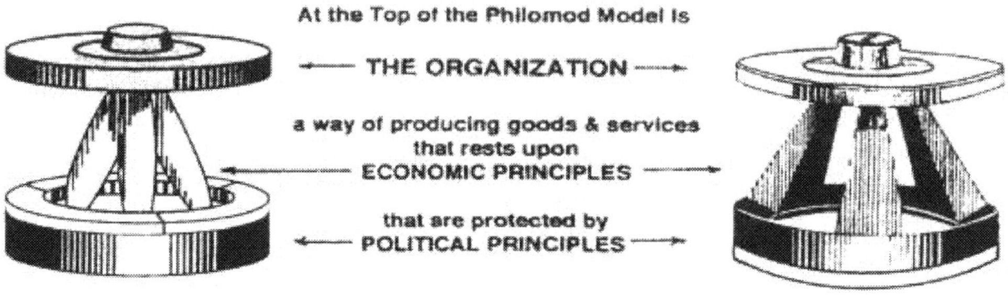

There Are 14 Principles

The Free-Market (FM) Principles Group

(1) Freedom of Individual Choice
(2) Freedom to Own (Private Ownership of Property)
(3) Freedom to Exchange (Competitive Markets)
(4) Freedom to Fund (Voluntary Funding)

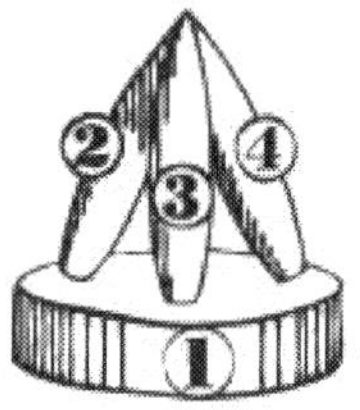

The Anti-Market [AM] Ideologies Group

[5] Centralized Governmental Power
[12] Governmental Ownership of Productive Property
[13] Controlled Markets (Restricted Exchange)
[14] Mandatory Funding (Taxation and Inflation)

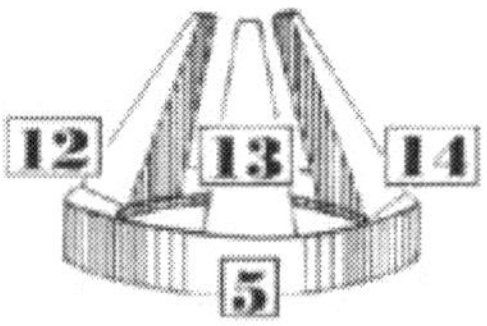

The Operating Organization

(7) Creativity and Innovation
(8) Management
(9) People Resources
(10) Property Resources
(11) The End-Product or Service

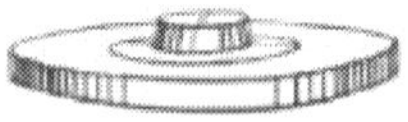

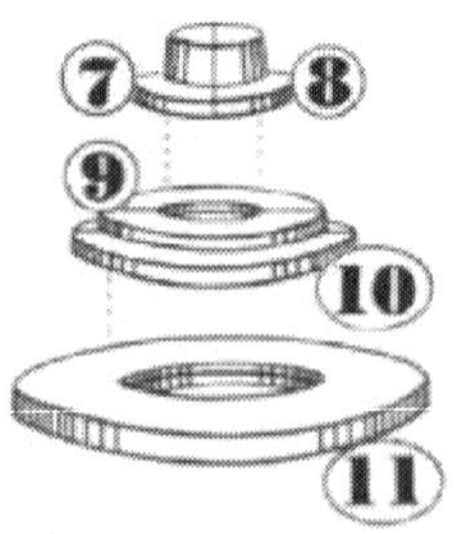

The Constitutional Balance of Governmental Power

[5] Centralized Governmental Power
(6) Limitation/Decentralization/Dispersion of Government Power
(1) Powers Reserved to the Individual

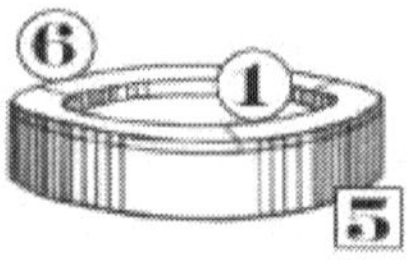

Interdependencies of 14 Political, Economic & Management Principles

Piece 1, Freedom of Individual Choice

Four Free Market Principles

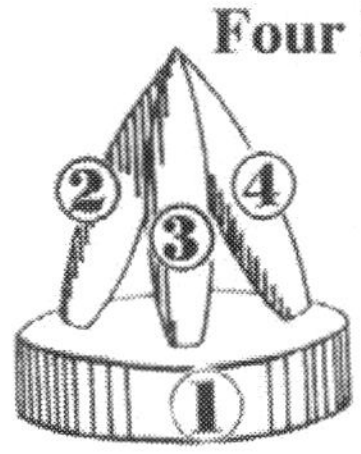

Pieces 2, 3 & 4, Freedoms to Own, Exchange & Fund, all based upon Piece 1, Freedom to Choose

Any Organization Anywhere

Piece 7, Creativity

Piece 8, Management

Piece 9, People Resources

Piece 10, Property Resources

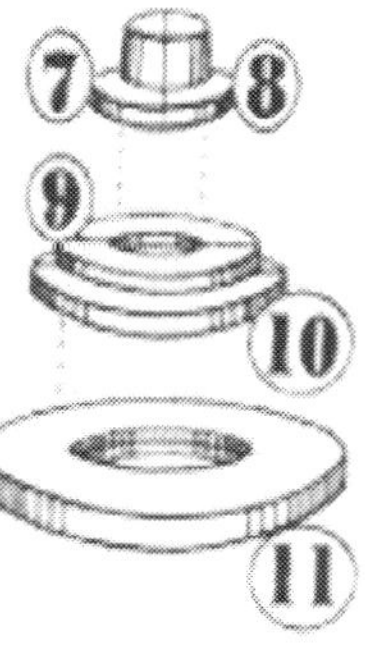

Piece 11, End-Product or Service

Enterprises

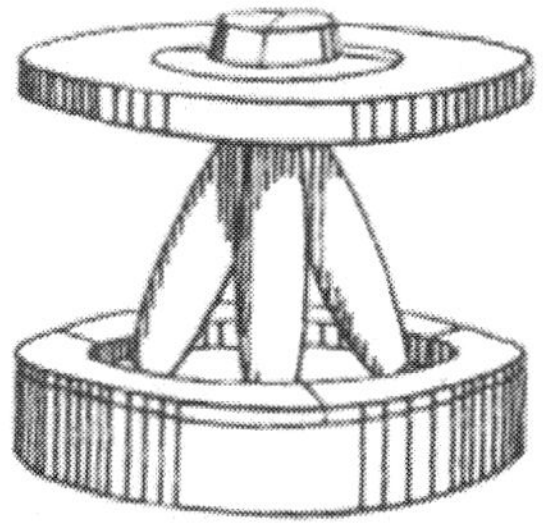

Organizations based on 4 Free-Market principles must produce a successful end-product or service, or they die.

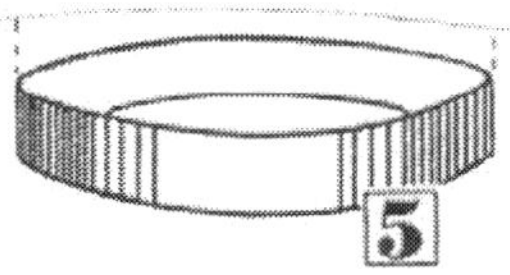

Piece 5, Centralized Governmental Power

Four Anti-Market Principles

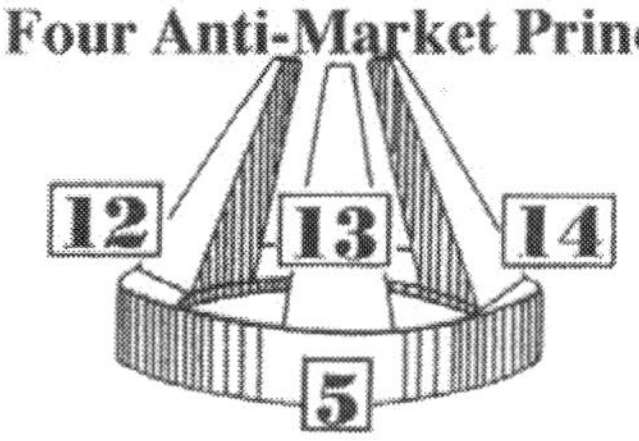

Pieces 12, 13, & 14, Government Ownership of Property, Controlled Exchange, and Funding by Force (Taxation), all based upon Piece 5, Centralized Governmental Power

Our Constitutional Protection

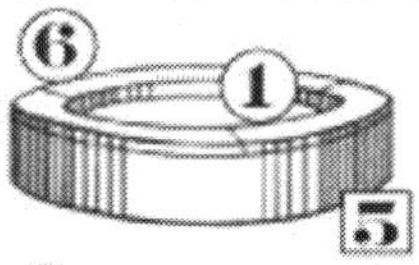

Piece 5, Governmental Power protects Piece 1, Freedom to Choose. Pieces 6, in 3 parts, Separation, Limitation and Decentralization of Power, protect Piece 1, Free Choice, from Piece 5.

Governmental Bureaus

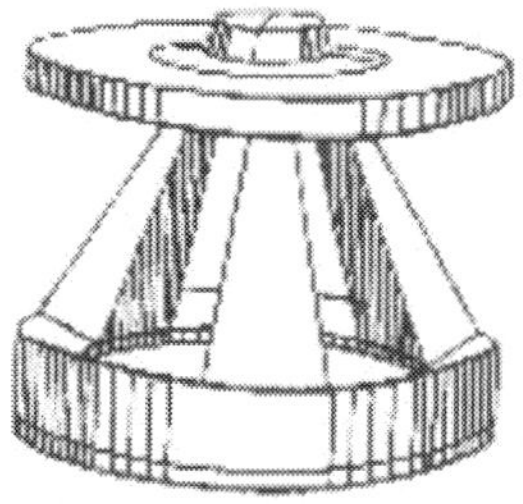

Organizations based on 4 Anti-Market principles can live forever whether they produce a successful end-product or not.

The product label, reproduced here, is affixed to the bottom of Piece 1. The ten Characteristics of Choice and the eight phases of the Choosing Process are repeated on each label as a handy reference for users.

Inside Bureaucracy & the Federal Register

You Asked Your Government to Improve the Situation? Here Are Your 79,435 Laws & Codes & Our $20 Trillion Debt

Let's go back to when you were at the "Creativity" and "Management" stages of forming your new organization. (You remember that all organizations in the Philomod Model are shaped like a wagon wheel.) You and your friends and associates *had the opportunity* to make a decision. You had the choice of putting your much-desired new organization atop one of two different groups of four principles: There was the *free-market basis with its three round legs with their feet planted in a disk,* your free-market choice. *You and your associates would tackle this challenge to improve your particular situation through your own actions.* Or, you and your group could choose to put your new organization, formed to improve your troublesome situation, atop *three square legs, allowing the Centralized Governmental Power ring as their base.*

You chose this second way to improve that situation that concerned you. What did you get when your efforts were successful at last?

Your "champion" or "point person" finally got the attention of a congressional committee. That committee in the Congress finally wrote a "bill" they believed would be the solution to your troublesome situation. A majority in the Congress then passed your "bill" and sent it over to the White House. The President, fresh off the golf course and aware that nothing too important was happening that day, signed your new bill and, zip, *your bill became the law of the land.* Happy Day! Then what happened? Governmental bureaucracy now moved into its usual low gear.

Inside Bureaucracy

Anthony Downs, in 1966, wrote *Inside Bureaucracy*, published by the Rand

Corporation. My copy has many little green post-its sticking out of its 290 pages. This little book has been more informative and helpful than almost any of the others in my small library. It ranks up there with my other favorites such as the works of Milton Friedman, Friedrich Hayek, and Peter Drucker. *Bureaucracy is the adversary of the American Free-Market system and the principles by which it operates. It is the Anti-Market. It is the entrepreneur's splitting headache. This is the "AM" vs. the "FM"*. There is the *free market,* and then there is the *anti-market*, the bureaucracy.

There is a free market-anti-market *ratio*. The FM-AM ratio tells us what percent of our nation's Gross Domestic Product *the government must take* for its operation. (The GDP is the value of all the goods and services that a nation produces.) In the past half century that ratio has been altered at an alarming rate. Philip K Howard of *Common Good* writes "There are over 140 million words of binding federal statutes and regulations, and states and municipalities add several billion more." (Wall Street Journal *"Starting Over with Regulation"* 12/2/11).

For 111 years after George Washington became our first president, the bureaucracy in the US *required only 3% of the GDP to conduct its affairs*. That was government's take in 1900. (Forbes article by Peter Brimelaw, March 15,1993). By Year 2011, our second 111 years, Centralized Governmental Power *took almost 40% of our GDP*. What is the *true* meaning of these statistics? They really mean this: *The 1900 American was a 97% free man. My father, age 10 in 1900, was 97% free. In this year, 2011, 111 years later, you and I are only 60% free. Been feeling like regulations are eating on you? You got that right.*

For the 111 years since 1900, with an almost 40% government control in the US *we are moving steadily toward 50%.* With future commitments for the continuation of Social Security, Medicare, and Medicaid, federal government programs *could within a few years consume 60% of our GDP. No one seems to know for sure.* Little wonder that Americans today are disappointed and disgusted with the Congress, the President and the Washington bureaucracy. *Now we're experiencing the burden of it all. We sense it. We hate it. Many fear it.*

From the early years in Europe, until the 1500s or thereabouts, it was accepted that feudal serfs, laboring on the lands of their lords, would hand over 50% of their annual crop or livestock production to his lordship. Serfdom meant their loss of 50% of the value of their labor. In the US as we approach a 50% level of taxation, think about Europe with some of its weaker nations like Greece facing *sovereign bankruptcy*. When that happens, it means no one will buy your government bonds, not even if you would pay them a 15% rate of interest or return. *Your government would now be of no value. It would be worthless. It is now stone cold broke.* But there may be worse considerations than worthlessness. *Like power... crushing power*! In his famous 1944 *"Road to Serfdom"* Friedrich Hayek wrote: In 1934 in Germany, the National Socialist Party, the Nazis, *needed to control only 53% of the GDP* **to control the German nation totally, absolutely.**

Today, 2011, Congressional "super-committees" in Washington are trying to find ways to reduce our debt. Again and again they fail. Why? Because a disturbing percentage of Americans still have the unbelievable guts to beg: "Ask the *government* to improve this situation." What happens to your new law, written to improve that situation of yours, passed by the Congress and signed by the President? Where does it go from the President's desk? To whom is it assigned for implementation?

It passes into the hands of the federal bureaucracy with this instruction: "Here is your new law. Now it is your job to write the rules and codes that will make it work."

Do new laws create an immediate interest within the hundreds of standing departments of the government bureaucracy? Indeed they do. The young ambitious bureaucrats try to get themselves moved to those departments to which the new laws have been assigned for action. There they can interpret the new law, spelling out the new rules for whomever must obey them. And Oh Boy! *That really improves their situation.*

Anthony Downs, in "*Inside Bureaucracy"* wrote that young bureaucrats see these as personal opportunities for themselves. They *seek to improve their situations,* to seize upon these to gain personal recognition and advancement. As years pass, the rules and codes implementing your new law have long since become old hat. That ambitious and knowledgeable young bureaucrat has long since moved on to more fertile ground.

Remaining behind in that old department, pushed off somewhere into the Virginia woods, are the old-timers. His or her attitude: "So some citizen thinks our old department isn't solving his problem? Tough! In two more years I've got retirement and that lovely government pension. Think I'm going to rock the boat? Let 'em scream and holler. I'm gonna be outa here." *This is what the Philomod demonstrates when it won't collapse.*
Downs wrote: "Even if a bureau cannot muster sufficient external support to continue as an autonomous agency, it might survive by getting some other aggrandizing bureau to swallow it. Most government bureaus disappear when the particular government that created them is replaced, as did Roman bureaus."

The Federal Register

We have the Federal Register to tell us how many hundreds of new laws were passed last year and each year before that, going back 75 years. "Ask the government to improve the situation?" In the Federal Register we get the answer with the resultant quantities of laws, codes, rules and regulations. The Federal Register is published by the Government Printing Office and is the official daily publication for rules, proposed rules, and notices of Federal agencies and organizations.

Here are six interesting facts provided us by the Office of the Federal Register, provided by Jim Hemphill, Special Assistant.

1 - Federal Register Act was approved on July 26, 1935

2 - First issue of the *Federal Register was published on March 16, 1936,* contained *eleven pages.*

3 - The largest annual edition of the *Federal Register* was published in 2008 and contained *79,435 pages.*

4 - In 2008 the *Federal Register* published a total of *31,879 documents*: Rules, Proposed Rules, Presidential Documents and Notices.

5 - During WWII, the number of documents printed jumped from 7,850 in FY 1941 to 18,569 in FY 1943, then returned closer to pre-war levels by FY1947.

6 - The *Federal Register* was placed online at www.gpoaccess.gov beginning in 1994 in response to GPO Access legislation. In 2009 GPO launched an improved website for searching its products, including the online *Federal Register*, at www.FDsys.gov. The online *Federal Register* is an official version of the publication.

Daniel Hannan, an elected member of the European Parliament and an admirer of the United States, writes this in "*The New Road to Serfdom*:"

> "The first shift in power happened under Theodore Roosevelt who, pleading the contingency of an active foreign policy, seized for the White House powers that had until then resided with the Congress and the states. It was he who began to make widespread use of executive decrees as an instrument of administration. Indeed the baleful statism of the second Roosevelt would not have been possible without the precedents established by the first."

The first few years of the 20th century, after Teddy Roosevelt's era, were pretty quiet. (The founding of the Internal Revenue Service and World War I being exceptions.) Then President Woodrow Wilson, formerly the President of Princeton University, threw in a few novel laws.

President Calvin Coolidge, "Silent Cal," in the 20's then provided several years of real relief. He even had the New England fortitude to assure us "The business of America is business." Then came the depression and Franklin D. Roosevelt, and Oh my! One of the first actions FDR took in 1932 when he came into office was to recognize the United Soviet Socialist Republic, which at the time had only been in existence for 19 years. Roosevelt had a kindly, fuzzy feeling toward socialism, apparently didn't want to keep Marx's and Lenin's people waiting for the blessings of the world's most free nation. It did not help their refractory minds.

In 1989, only 70 years after their 1919 revolution, they had to became "Russia" all over again. Some new nations, particularly those being governed by socialist theory, they found, just can't hack it. Even the blessings of the president of *a superior well-established 200-year-old nation* had not been enough to save them. Even today in 2011, Russia still has the deadly iron collar of its failed socialist beliefs around its neck. Its understanding of entrepreneurship is somewhere between none-at-all and primitive. That degree of entrepreneurial understanding might also be said of some members of our U.S. Congress.

Taking the All-Languages Philomod(R) Model Global
As They Move West, Young Islamics Can See the Benefits, the Prosperity and the Wealth Free-Market Systems Offer. Are These the New "Westward Pioneers?"

Population Sizes of the Christian and Islamic Worlds (Wikipedia)

Christianity	2,059 Million	32%	(dropping)
Islam	1,226 Million	19%	(growing)

An Arab Professor of Sociology provides us some opening insights:

"The concept of freedom in the Arab world is synonymous with disorder," writes Fatima Mernissi, an Arab and professor of sociology at Mohammed V University in Morocco. She writes: "When I visit a Muslim country, whether Pakistan or Egypt or Algeria, what strikes me as a sociologist is first of all the strong feeling of bitterness in the people-- the intellectuals, the young, peasants. I see bitterness over blocked ambition, over frustrated desires for consumption--of clothes, commodities, and gadgets, but also of cultural products like books and quality films and performances that give meaning to life and reconcile the individual with his environment and his country. In no Western country have I ever seen such intense bitterness over wasted talent, spoiled chances, inequality of opportunity, or absurd career blockage."

"We cannot," she writes, "continue to stifle the imagination, the freedom to ponder and dream, for that is the locus of invention the source of wealth in the electronic age." (Islam and Democracy…Fear of the Modern World, by Fatima Mernissi (Addison-Wesley, Reading MA, 1992,))

Our story begins...

An American and an Arab meet in the desert...

Neither senses a feeling of antagonism. No reason to; their countries are at peace. This is simply one stranger about to meet another. From some 25 paces each studies facial expressions of the other. Two rather reasonably handsome masculine faces.

When three paces apart they stop. The Arab picks up a small stick. Bending forward he draws a curved line in the sand.

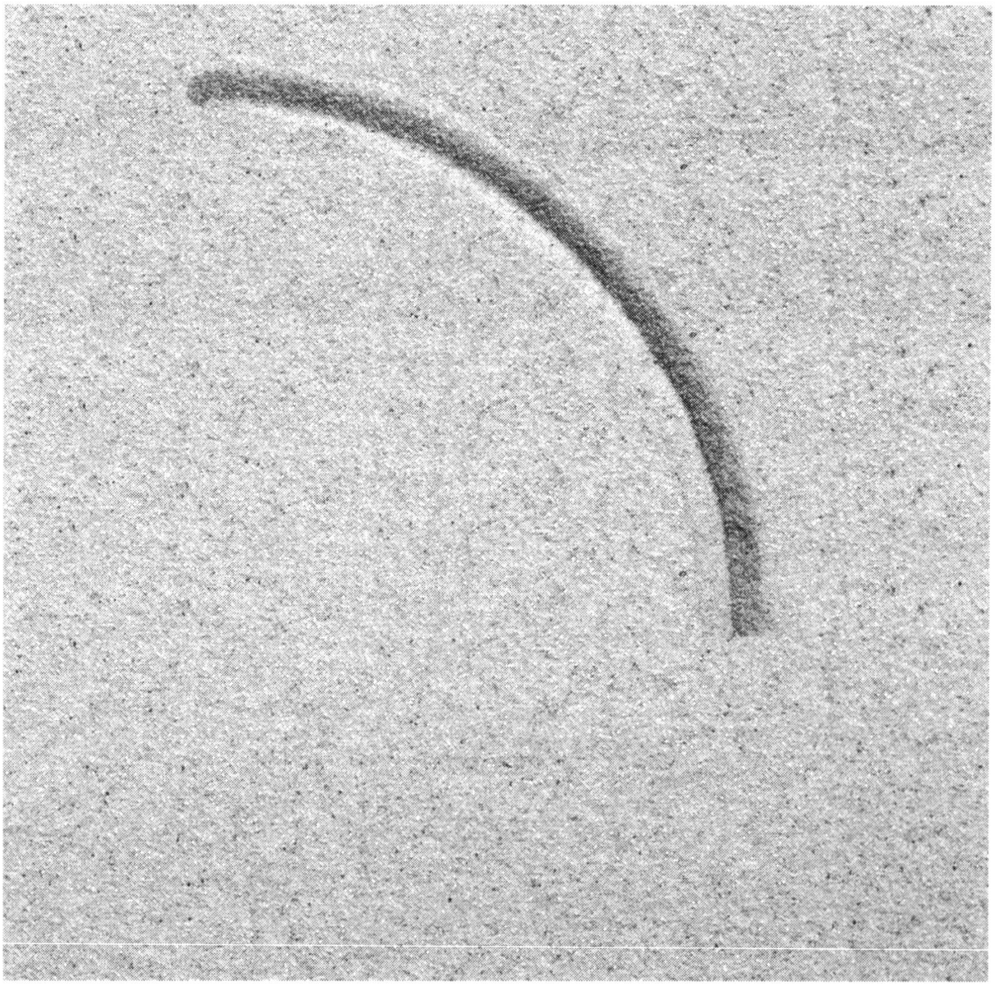

Today, at this moment, he seeks an answer from this Westerner to an important question. The American knows the procedure. If he draws another curved line across that of the Arab's, it will be the sign of the fish, St.Peter's sign, a Christian sign, a missionary's sign, not the symbol the Arab hopes to see this day. If the American draws another curved line with one end touching the Arab's line, it will indicate that their meeting has a different objective. The Muslim watches. The American draws a second curved line with one end meeting the Arab's line.

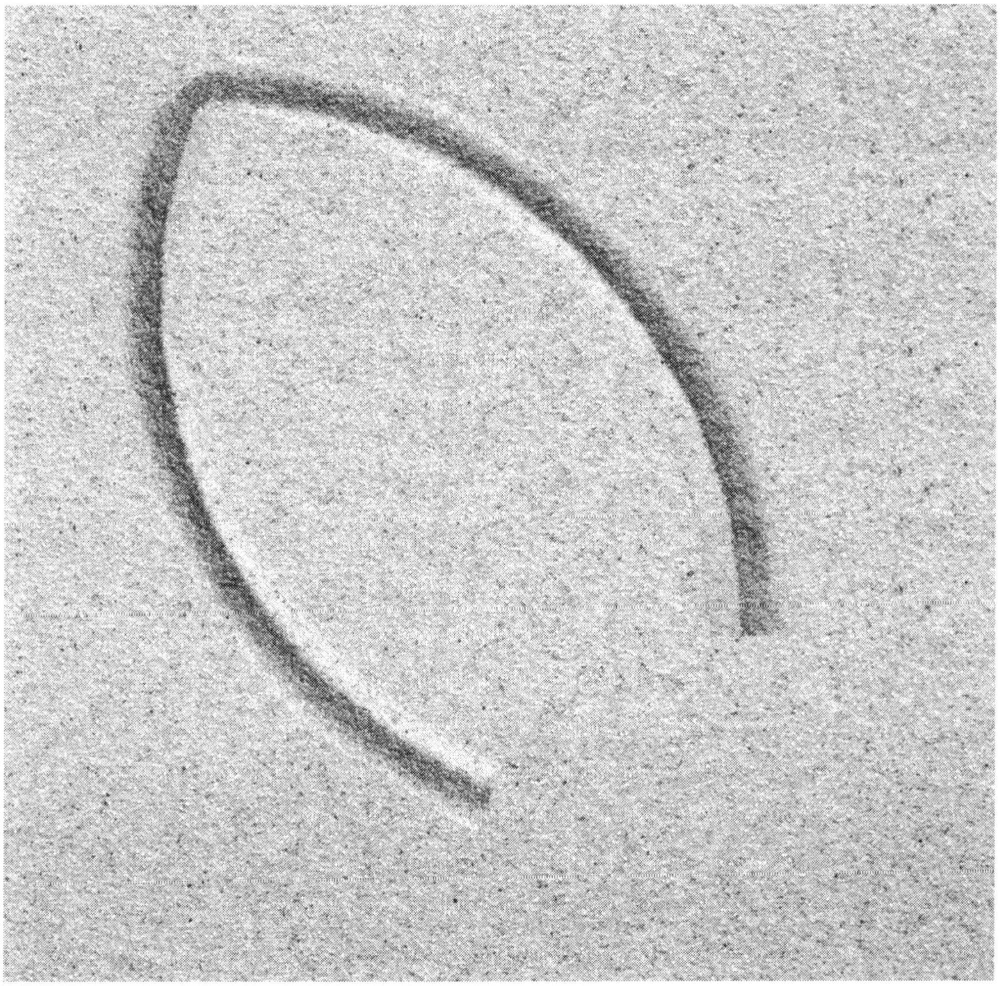

The Arab draws a third line.

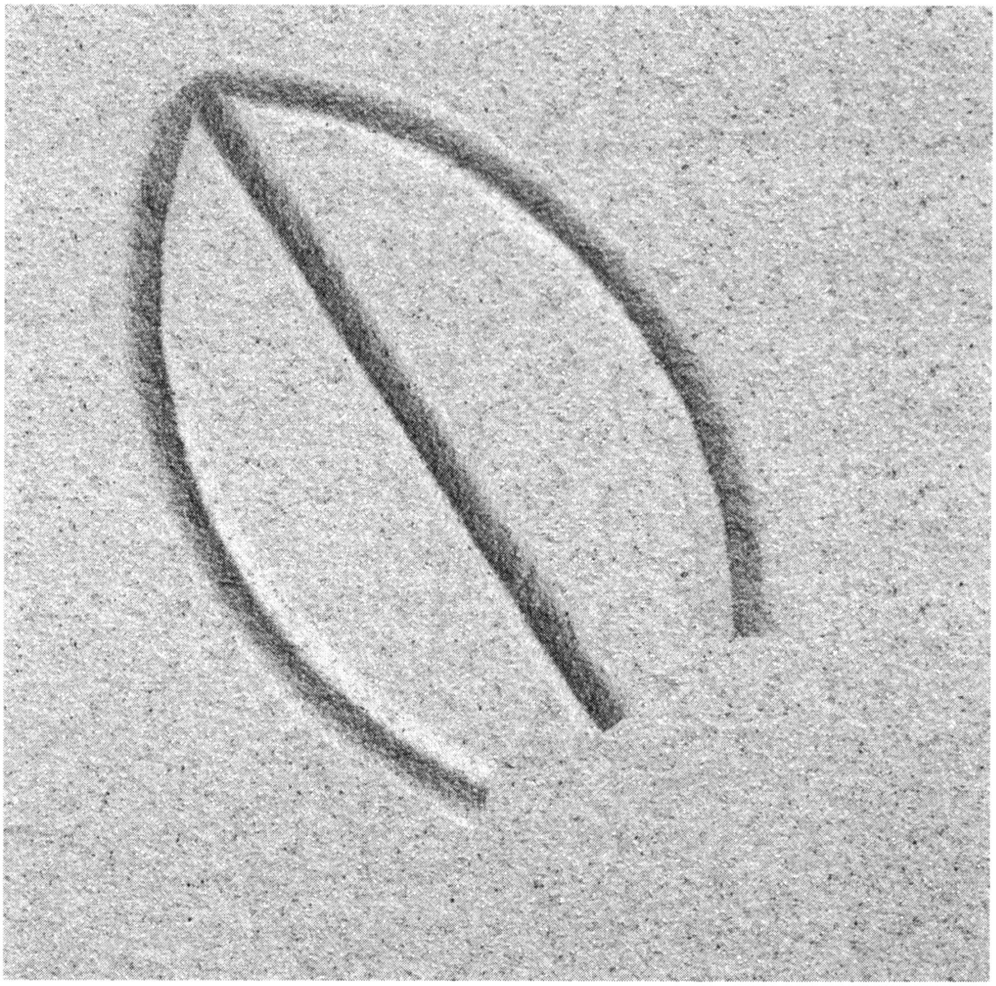

The American smiles and draws a circle beneath the three lines.

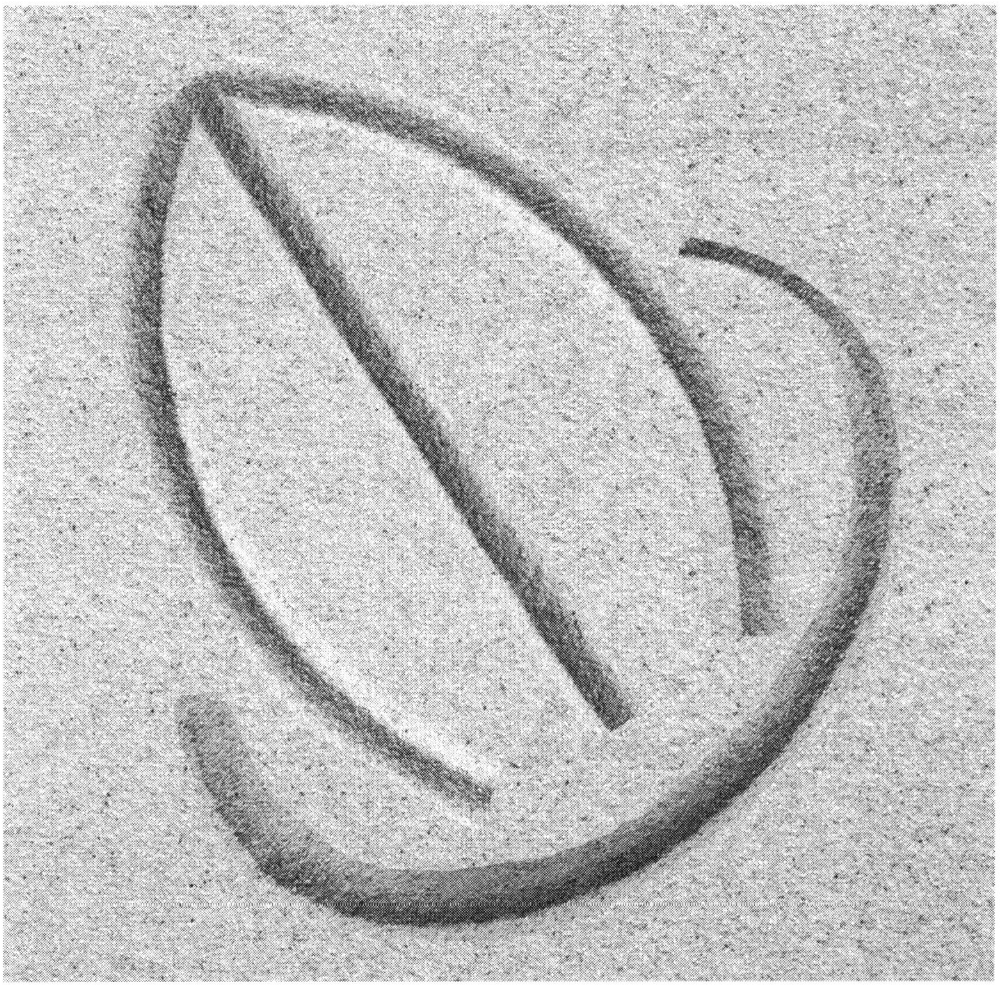

The Arab smiles, both are now at ease, because today they will not be talking about religion. They have drawn a Freepod in the sand. They will talk about a wooden model. Today they will talk about a wooden model and the "free market," a neutral subject, new to the Muslim, very familiar to the westerner.

The men shake hands.

"What is your name?"

"Mohammed. And yours?"

"Sam." The American picks up his rucksack.

Together they start toward the village. It is a new subject of interest to the Arab.

A friend suggested to him that this is the idea that made America prosperous. The Muslim has heard talk, he has heard that this is a not a subject to place him on the defensive. It is a philosophy that many Muslims, particularly those living in America, have found very helpful even though not completely in keeping with every single one of the Koran's teachings. These far-off relatives have not found it offensive. They have found it thought provoking and useful. There lies the key.

At a shaded table in the village, as they take seats at their benches, three other Arab men approach and sit down. The Arab introduces his friends to the American. The men, it appears, know a small amount of English. Marc, Mohammed's cousin knows a bit more than the others. Not much, but with help from expressive hands and facial changes, they will communicate passably well in Pidgin English. It has aided primitive communications for centuries.

The American places his rucksack on the table, opens it, and takes out five pieces of a well-worn Philomod model, the five principles that define all organizations. His audience displays interest, almost an eager anticipation. Sam begins with the five pieces or principles of every organization, the wagon-wheel-shaped group.

"Everyone faces situations that trouble them. We use our imaginations to seek ideas to deal with these situations." He holds one of the smallest pieces in his hand. He looks at the cousin. "This little piece, (he holds Piece #7) represents "creativity and innovation."' He looks toward Marc, "Do you have a pick-up truck?"

"I do."

"Did your grandfather have a pick-up truck?"

Cousin laughs. "No, he and his friends had a camel."

"Then the pick-up truck was something new in your family. Someone had created something new."

"Oh, yes."

"Did the pick-up improve their situation?

Yes. Hauled more things. Goes faster, more fun. Doesn't spit at you."

They were interrupted by one of the men. In Arabic they discussed what had been said. Then they were quiet again.

Sam: "I notice you wear a wristwatch."

"Yes."

"Did your grandfather wear a watch?"

"No, but he might have had a watch in his pants pocket."

"Then the wristwatch was an improvement over his situation?'

"Oh yes, you just look at your arm and there is the time of day."

"Did your great, great grandfather have a watch in his pocket?"

"No," Marc answered, "No one had watches then. Those were the olden days. Then the time of day did not interest people that much. In a few villages there was a sundial near the village well. That was all they needed."

"So," Sam said, "we are talking about creating something new. In the wristwatch over the pocket watch, we are talking about an improvement in something old. That's what this little piece in our model stands for: It stands for a new idea or an improvement on an old idea. It stands for an idea that might improve the situation."

Once again, the men converse in Arabic.

Three hours pass quickly. Piece by piece, *principle by principle*, the simple lessons continue. Then with interest lagging and each man needing to attend to his prayers and chores, the little group agrees to meet again. Same time, same place tomorrow. Sam is pleased. He has opened the door just a crack. He hopes, over the next few days, they can cover several of the Philomod's pieces, *its principles. Free-market principles.*

But he remembers that Muslim nations also have a Centralized Governmental Power (CGP) *a combination of their church and government.* He knew who would soon be coming to their table. The village's imam would have questions. While the Koran seems to prefer no special form of government, the imam would seek assurance that passages in the Koran were not being ignored or violated. These were questions one had to expect. What he was ready to give to the imam were twenty testimonials, printed in Arabic, from Muslim families now living in Germany, France, and America. These Muslim families (whose names and locations would not been revealed in their stories in the little booklet) in 2011 were now *at ease with the ideas of the free market,* carried on with their daily duties and prayers. No problems. *Their minds seemed comfortable.*

(As a part of these small booklets in Arabic, a short list of Translations of Key Words and Phrases from English into Arabic should be included. Perhaps 40 to 50 words and phrases will be sufficient, but these would also tend to give comfort to anxious minds. These terms will also help any translators whose assistance may be called upon because of an unfamiliar territory.)

Over the next several months Sam helped Mohammed and Marc with their first joint project: a small map of the area with the names and locations of each village within a radius of 50 miles. Sam in his travels realized that no such localized maps existed. For centuries there had been caravans of commerce throughout the region, and the villagers in one area had heard tales of their neighbors in nearby villages. Were these nearby or far away? No one was sure.

Sam and his new friends approached an important caliph. Could funds be found to finance a series of star shoots with navigational instruments to determine the exact geographical location of each of about 50 villages? This was the caliph's domain. He saw the political advantages immediately. It would offer him opportunities to better manage his own areas of political influence. The funds were found, geographers with their sextants were engaged to come and carry out the project.

Seven months later, the first detailed maps of roughly a hundred-square-mile area were completed and published. What a hit! "Look! There is Village X. I used to go there as a child. I believe I may have relatives there. It is only 28 kilometers south of here. I will talk with my wife about a little trip to visit there. Next week we'll buy gas for the pick-up and go."

The first step in a new era had been taken. Sam and his new associates had found a way to improve the quality of life, *improve the situation* for hundreds of local Muslims. The people also found the new map *improved commerce* between dozens of villages. The caliph was pleased.

HERE ENDS OUR FICTITIOUS STORY.

In America in 2011, we are not yet prepared to send young men alone into a foreign, often dangerous Islamic world. We do, however, have a new educational tool. Our Philomod Model is an invaluable assist to foreign language translators. It helps them introduce and explain extremely abstract political, economic and management concepts.

With a people who have never seen a computer, people who may not yet have electricity, your visual aids must not only be visible, but *tangible, three dimensional, and hand-held.* With the cooperation of Mohammed, Marc *and the imam*, our hero Sam made rapid progress. But we cannot allow a fictitious story to set us off on frivolous journeys.

A Plea About Religion

Religion-- Christian, Muslim, Jewish, Buddhist, whatever-- need not, should not, be brought into studies and discussions of political-economic beliefs and theory. Political-economic principles, freedom principles and the principles of power can be explored completely independently of religious principles. In fact, it is a must. Only when it is approached as an independent philosophical subject can it be expected to develop its own themes, to do its work globally, to accomplish that of which it is capable.

Political economic freedom improves situations, brings wealth and prosperity. In their own ways, the freedoms to choose, to own, to exchange and to fund *will work.* To Christians, Muslims, Jews or Buddhists: you have your faiths and established ways. You have had your centuries of wars, successes and failures, independent for the most part of economic teachings. Let economic exploration, discussion and three-dimensional models move ahead on their own independent merits.

Now let's shift gears. Different time period. Different nation.

Let's drop back several hundred years to the Catholic church in Italy. The church had always been the central passion in life. Poor men living in stone hovels devoted 14 hours of their days building magnificent cathedrals in the name of their Christ, their popes, and their saints. Today these structures are the centerpieces of many American tourists' visits to the European continent. We are awed by the workmanship and beauty these stone masons and sculptors created.

Early there were parallels between Roman Catholicism and Islam.

1 - The only way to heaven was through their priests and the mullahs.

2 - Only the clergy could interpret the scriptures.

3 - Religious law - canon or sharia - trumped civil law.

4 - Separation of Church and State only when the State forced it.

After the printing press was invented, over the years books became cheaper and more widely circulated. Thousands then millions learned to read. More could interpret the scriptures themselves rather than having to depend upon their priests and mullahs.

The history of the Catholic religion in Italy is of special interest to us. From the 1200s to the 1800s, as government became less an instrument of the Church, and as people began to learn to read and could interpret the scriptures for themselves; the Italian people began to modify their outlooks. *Without being less religious* they found that they paid more attention to *improving their situations.* They began to differentiate. Their church could be a matter of *their religion* and improving the *daily necessities of living* could be seen as a *separate matter of sociology and economics. Apparently, they discovered, there was no conflict.* As time passed, this acceptability grew ever more comfortable.

Islam, *while a religion, is also Centralized Governmental Power.* In the 20th century Muslim families, *as immigrants*, set about improving their situations as millions *moved westward* -- "moving westward," that has a familiar American ring to it, doesn't it?-- sought refuge in Germany, France, and Great Britain They are learning that *freedom of worship is accepted alongside economic freedom.* Many, since we promise not to identify them, we hope will be generous with their stories. This defining of the two different roles should clarify and help. *There is no conflict. There is only an improvement in their overall situations.*

These westward bound immigrants of today have the personal testimonials we seek: In two words...*It works*. These families' stories in simple booklet form in English, Arabic and Hindi-Urdu will be for the "Philomod Ambassadors" to distribute. As a supplement in these booklets there should be included in the Arabic and Hindi-Urdu translation of the English terms that help clarify, simplify and define the most commonly used terms of economics and sociology. Our State Department should lend us their assistance. *The ice does not need to be broken. It has already been broken.*

American church congregations send their missionaries abroad every week. Probably the most successful are the young Mormon men who go aboard in pairs. Every day for two years, these young men face strangers, dangers, and homesickness. How do they do it?

We are interested in sending young men abroad with Philomod Models rather than crosses. How in the world can these entrepreneurial opportunities be approached?

It can be done.

To you foundations throughout the US, Europe and South America interested in the promotion and expansion of the free-market philosophy: Heritage, Cato, Hoover, American Enterprise Institute. (You know who you are). Worthwhile projects, as you know, *can boost your financial support.* A visual, tactile, three-dimensional teaching tool, clarifying free-market principles; *has never been available before. That's big news.*

Your major business leaders, *fed up with bureaucracy*, want to hear that good news! *They will back you.* One of their million-dollar contributions might send eight men into the field with the finest selling tools for freedom ever available. Send *your own free-market ambassadors out into the world.* Unleash your own star performers from their desk-bound lives.

You now know that our little model clarifies the free-market philosophy through a universally welcomed medium, a three-dimensional classroom and lecture-circuit teaching aid. Its pieces are principles, the principles that *improve the situation and deliver prosperity and wealth. Look at the quality of the people who have enthusiastically endorsed it.*

Philomod Institute has your kit of materials in a rucksack standing ready. Available for any foundation or institution, we hope to develop a one-week training course. You can name your candidates for this course in "Ambassadors for Enterprise" and we will see that the people you have selected are brought together in a convenient central location. You, as their sponsors, will be responsible for their transportation, hotels and meals. We will be responsible for their update in Free-markets and Anti-markets.

Proposed Five-Day Training Course Outline (subject to modification)

Mon	Public Relations, Guiding Principles. Salesmanship Refresher. Entrepreneurial highlights in US history: Declaration of 1774, Constitutional Convention 1787, Federal legislation effecting free markets 1789 - 2010. Homework: Acquaint selves with Philomod Model.
Tues	Review US Pol-Ec highlights. Devote all day to Philomod Model. Ten Characteristics of Choice, Eight steps of Choosing Process. Two Basic Structures: Free-Market and Anti-Market. 14 Pieces or Principles comprising two basic structures. Individual practice presentations.
Wed	Philomod Model quiz. Islamic nations, principle languages, variations in wealth & prosperity, characteristics, dress. Highlights of Muslim religion. Common elements: prayers, mosques, mullahs, imams, caliphs & ayatollahs. Annual events & holidays. Common practices, Essentials of Muslim etiquette.
Thurs	Written exam: Muslim highlights. Philomod presentations. Presentation tips and critiques. US State Dept. representatives provide current affairs info on Muslim territories, political persons of importance, who is most approachable. Highlight current travel conditions in each rep's territory.
Fri	Travel dress & tips. Finding room & board. Making contacts with community leaders. Cell phone use, when available. Being always easy for others to reach. Expense accounts & record keeping, by notebook or computer. Processing sales orders, warehousing when necessary. Evaluating, hiring, and paying translators. Final Exam

Graduates of these classes are now Ambassadors and Clarifiers of the Free-Market Philosophy. They will also be the *sales representatives* for that philosophy. We would expect their sponsoring institutions to cover their travel, meals, and accommodations expenses. *Philanthropic foundations however, in order to maintain the tax-free identities of the sponsoring foundation, are not allowed to receive compensation from commercial ventures.*

Ways must be found for these ambassadors to also distribute Philomod products in their territories.

Here's an idea. Have you moved to the United States over the past several years and done quite well? Do you feel that you would like friends or relatives in the "old country" to come here and share in these advantages you have been able to capitalize upon? A friend in Africa, Asia, Eastern Europe or Central America? Or would it be better that they remain there and use our proven principles to build a better life? Philomod Institute will open its classes to others seeking to be "Free-Enterprise Ambassadors." Learn the basics, go back to the home country, and teach the principles.

Philomod Institute will offer this program as the designer, manufacturer, and marketer of a high-quality copyrighted, trademarked, global teaching aid. We believe sales incentives are always an essential asset in good overall marketing practices. Once again, *there have been no global tools. And symbols are vitally important.* The flags of different nations, *their nation's symbols*, may offend other people of other nations. When riled up they may express their emotions by burning the stars and stripes or other nations' flags.

This brings us to another objective I would like to discuss with you. This, I know you will understand, is a *secondary* objective. Our *first* objective remains the education of the American teen, who has been brutally short-changed by our government. Thirty million youngsters between the ages of 13 and 21 have absolutely no idea of our American free-market philosophy. With our Philomod Model and this book we have made two tools available to you parents of these teens, tools that "show and tell." Our model shows. Our book tells. These tools make it easy to give your youngsters the education they have been denied.

(Nor should parents who have placed their teen-agers in private Eastern prep schools assume that American free-market principles are being emphasized. Here are schools where parents should have their say.) You can advance your son or daughter *five years ahead of their classmates.* You will also set your children out onto that positive path our Founding Fathers intended for all of us.

One hundred years ago my father took Goodyear "global," One way to begin taking the Philomod Model global is by spreading the *symbol* of our model. This:

This is what entrepreneurs do. Take an idea that seems to have promise, and develop that idea into a product that will *improve the situation* of a group of people.

Our USA has now had an unbeatable reputation for prosperity for several hundred years. For this reason foreigners still flock to our shore, both legally and illegally. There has never been a universal symbol that everywhere on this globe clarifies the four free-market principles that built today's USA. Literally, the stripes in our US flag stand for the 13 original states, and the stars in the blue field stand for the current number of 50 states.

Burners of the US flag are trying to burn what they believe is America. Many Muslims see us as corrupt, as standing in the way of their god. Our prosperity and wealth are looked upon as illegitimate because they have not been brought about through their beliefs.

Germany's National Socialist Party – the Nazis – promoted its symbol, the swastika, with all the governmental strength they could possibly put behind it. But when their nation was defeated, this symbol dried up and went away, hopefully forever.

The Soviets tried to promote socialism. Again the strengths of Lenin and Stalin with all their power put everything they had behind the effort, but when, after 70 years their socialist philosophy proved worthless, this symbol also failed.

The Freepod fills a global void. As a symbol how can we begin to make it universal? It depicts those four freedoms that have always promoted prosperity, the Freedoms to Choose, to Own, to Trade, and to Fund. It can say to the world: "You people don't need to come to the USA. This is how we did it and still do it. You can do it too!" Nobel Laureate Friedrich Hayek said it this way: *"Liberty is a system under which all government action is guided by principles."*

The Freepod symbol clarifies, simplifies, and dramatizes principles. Kind reader, here is a question for you. Where and in what ways can this new symbol be promoted? We don't have a Hitler or a Stalin to force our symbol onto the world. And thank God for that. We must do it voluntarily.

Here is one idea a friend suggested: Ask America's big global corporations to print the Freepod symbol in the lower left hand corner of all their company stationary. That would spark people's curiosity. Good idea! Let's not ignore this worldwide opportunity any longer. *Let's get started. Shout out our four basic freedoms! Spread our NEW SYMBOL!*

Have ideas? Send them to us. *Let's get our global freedom symbol rolling!*

Go Team!

But before we part company, another question comes to mind: Do you think the Arabs and their Muslim brethren *will ever have fun being entrepreneurs?* Perhaps the Saudi princes offer us a clue. They have certainly built many exciting buildings and designed beautifully modern cities. Perhaps those actions answer our question.

Personally, I would like to catch a flight out of New York for Dubai in the United Arab Emirates to watch the Formula Ones zip around their new racecourse there. Think the Arabs are having as much fun as we used to have back in Indiana, when we went to Indianapolis on Memorial Day to see the "500"?

I can remember the great Argentine champion, Juan Fangio, and this is a true story. I saw Fangio, dressed in his double-breasted business suit, no flame-retardant suit for him, slip on a helmet, get into his Ferrari (or Maserati) and in less than 90 seconds was up to 200 miles an hour doing practice laps. *Business suit -- just another day in his office!* I was standing on the inside of the Indianapolis oval right next to the track and turned to my friend to ask, "Can you believe that?"

His answer: "For Pete's sake Bob, never, *never* turn your back on a race car!"

Robert E. Sonntag

1980 was a wonderful year. We closed our Kon-Tiki Resorts on 4,500 feet of oceanfront at St. Augustine Beach. There are now 1,200 condominiums there. Finally, I would have the time to study economics, not included in our journalism courses at Chapel Hill.

As I began building a library on the subject, I became increasingly frustrated and dissatisfied with its absence of simplicity and clarity. My "Madison Avenue type" mind sought a *primer. How can you sell an idea you cannot clarify?* It should be made as simple as "*show and tell.*" What were the basic ideas, and then the building blocks of conservative American political-economics?

Finally I found the "Austrians," Ludwig von Mises, Friedrich Hayek, Peter Drucker, Hans Sennholz, and the great Milton Friedman. From their lectures and writings I learned that there are Principles of Freedom and of Force.

Political-economics, I found, could indeed be boiled down into a primer:

a – There are 10 Characteristics of Free Choice: First two: 1) Improve the situation. 2) Choices come in twos or more. A choice of one is Force.

b – Hayek pointed out there are two Systems; A "Free-Market System" and (my name for it) an "Anti-Market System."

c – Only 14 Basic Principles (or pieces) can convey a good understanding.

It took five years to complete the Philomod® Model's design, the "building blocks." The blueprints were copyrighted March 10, 1986. They then went to a wonderful wood-working factory in Vermont. This book took a little longer.

PHILOMOD® INSTITUTE, INC.
4358 Timuquana Road, Unit 126, Jacksonville FL 32210 USA
philomod.com resonntag@earthlink.net

Made in United States
Orlando, FL
04 November 2026

90202045R00074